SPIRAL GUIDES

Travel with Someone You Trust ®

LONDON

Contents

Written by Lesley Reader
Magazine by Fiona Dunlop
Where to sections by Elizabeth Carter
Captions and additional writing by Tim Jepson

Copy edited by Lodestone Publishing
Page layout by Amanda Chauhan, Tony Truscott
Verified by Paul Murphy
Indexed by Marie Lorimer

Edited, designed and produced by AA Publishing
Published in the United States by AAA Publishing,
1000 AAA Drive, Heathrow, Florida 32746
Published in the United Kingdom by AA Publishing

ISBN 1-56251-673–6
Mapping produced by the Cartographic Department of
the Automobile Association

Color separation by Leo Reprographics
Printed and bound in China by Leo Paper Products

10 9 8 7 6 5 4 3 2 1

London
the magazine

Double Destruction

London's two infernal nightmares, the Great Fire and the Blitz, albeit three centuries apart, both left smoldering ruins. Yet, phoenix-like, out of the ashes arose new approaches to urban living that transformed the face of the capital.

London's Burning!

The flames crackled and cinders whirled into the night sky: It was September 2, 1666, the king's bakery in Pudding Lane was on fire and 80 percent of the city of London was about to go up in smoke. It was not the first time this medieval town had seen a fire, but this one was to be by far the most destructive. As the flames raged, the Lord Mayor dithered, unwilling to rouse himself, and announced dismissively that "a woman might piss it out." That woman unfortunately did not materialize, and the fire soon spread to riverside warehouses filled with combustible materials. The blaze took hold.

Even the efforts of King Charles II, his brother the Duke of York and armies of fire-fighters were to little avail and four nights later, when the wind

The Great Fire of London, 1666

abated and the fire finally died down, over 13,000 houses had bitten the dust, along with 76 churches, 44 livery company halls, the Guildhall, the Royal Exchange and St. Paul's Cathedral. Remarkably, there were only nine deaths, but 100,000 became homeless.

It didn't take long for the king to issue new building regulations: All new construction was to be in brick or stone and all streets were to be wide enough for carriages to pass along them. This Rebuilding Act was the first of much legislation over the next two centuries designed to regulate the standard of housing. Although Sir Christopher Wren's plan for a model urban layout was rejected, on grounds of practicality, some improvements were made, notably a continuous quay between the Tower of London and London Bridge.

Rebuilding took about ten years, not counting St. Paul's and 50 or so churches, all designed by Wren – but the most important spinoff was the accelerated drift to the suburbs, either across the river to Southwark or west to Westminster. The old City of London thus lost its hold, its population plummeted, and the embryo of suburban London took shape.

Survivors

Not every City church succumbed to the flames of the Great Fire. Among the survivors in the Bishopsgate area were St.-Botolph-without-Bishopsgate, the tiny St. Ethelburga and above all the remarkable St. Helen's, once part of a 12th-century Benedictine nunnery. However, all three were to suffer extensive damage in 1993 when an IRA bomb blasted out Bishopsgate. To the west, the beautiful medieval church of St.-Bartholomew-the-Great, much restored in the 19th century, also escaped the fire, together with London's oldest hospital, St. Bartholomews ("Barts").

Sir Christopher Wren, architect of St. Paul's Cathedral and some 50 London churches

Although thousands of steel bomb shelters were issued to Londoners who had gardens, many East Enders used the public shelters. The largest was an underground goods yard in Stepney, where 16,000 people would spend their nights in overcrowded conditions. Far better in terms of facilities was a network of caverns at Chislehurst, Kent, where electric light, bunk-beds, toilets and an old piano all added to the rousing atmosphere of solidarity. But top of the popularity stakes were the Underground stations. Tickets were issued for regulars, bunk-beds set up and impromptu sing-alongs took place. At times, around 177,000 people came here each night.

London Blitz

Blackouts and wailing sirens were the prelude to London's World War II drama: the Blitz. The aerial assault of the city began on September 7, 1940, when some 320 Luftwaffe bombers flew up the Thames to unleash their devastation on the East End. The bombing continued mercilessly for 57 consecutive nights, then intermittently for a further six months, with more than 27,000 bombs and countless incendiaries dropped on the city. By November more than 11,000 people had been killed and 250,000 were homeless. Initially the East End, Docklands and the City were the targets, but attacks on central London soon followed. The last raid came on May 10, 1941, when 550 bombers hammered the capital for five hours, destroying the Chamber of the House of Commons (among other buildings) and killing more than 1,400 people.

After the war, priority was given to planning new satellite towns and filling the craters that pockmarked the urban landscape. The late 1950s and 1960s witnessed a building bonanza of offices and public housing, with tower blocks often overshadowing a Wren church or a Regency terrace. Slum clearance, too, gave way to highrises, but it took two decades and inner city riots during the 1980s before these concrete jungles were recognized as nonviable. Like them or not, they're part of London's history and have created a social patchwork across the capital.

In the last-ditch Nazi assault of 1944 terrifying V1 doodlebugs (flying bombs) were launched from northern France, soon followed by the even faster and more devastating V2 rockets. It was impossible to mount a defense against these rockets and they killed more than 2,000 Londoners.

St. Paul's Cathedral, a miraculous survivor of the London Blitz

In 1999 a memorial to the 30,000 Londoners who died in the Blitz was unveiled by the Queen Mother in the courtyard of St. Paul's Cathedral. She was an appropriate choice to dedicate the memorial. At the height of wartime bombing, she had tirelessly toured the city's bombsites. When Buckingham Palace received a direct hit, she wrote: "I'm glad we've been bombed. It makes me feel I can look the East End in the face."

THE FACTS OF LONDON LIFE

London, Europe's largest city, covers more than 610 square miles

The city attracts around 29 million visitors each year, and despite the capital's 95,000 hotel rooms, it is estimated that 20,000 more beds are needed to keep up with demand.

Daytime traffic crawls at an average speed of 10 mph through the city's streets. No wonder every day around 5 million people opt to use the Underground (Tube).

Westminster, the most visited part of the capital, has around 90 tonnes of trash collected from its streets each day.

London's population today, hovering around the 7 million mark, is the same as it was in 1900 when it was the world's most populated city.

The city's financial institutions process about $300 billion in foreign exchange daily and manage half the world's ship brokering, company mergers and acquisitions.

The Millennium Dome, the largest structure of its kind in the world, could accommodate Nelson's Column standing upright and the Eiffel Tower placed horizontally.

One-third of Londoners live alone.

The city has 1,700 parks in an area of around 70 square miles and it's possible to walk from Westminster to Notting Hill, a distance of 2 miles, through parkland alone.

The Millennium Bridge connecting Tate Modern with St. Paul's Cathedral is the first pedestrian bridge to be built across the Thames since 1900.

At the height of the recession in 1992, the freshly completed but unoccupied Canary Wharf was losing $55 million per day.

There are 40,000 tulips planted each year in front of Buckingham Palace and 250,000 more at Hampton Court.

The 1,020-foot (311-m) length of Canary Wharf station is enough to accommodate the adjacent Canary Wharf Tower, Britain's tallest building, placed horizontally.

Battersea Dogs Home is the world's oldest rescue centre for lost or unwanted dogs.

Canary Wharf Tower, at the heart of the Docklands redevelopment, is nowadays fully occupied

Tracking down the glitterati

Literary, Artsy, Musical, Political or Thinking London... the metropolis bristles with blue plaques posted on the former residences of its illustrious inhabitants. Today, with well-defined areas still attracting high-profile personalities, you may just bump into a living legend. London is constantly evolving, so you are unlikely still to see cutting-edge artists in upscale Hampstead or Chelsea. Increasing property values have sent them running to Hackney, whose lofts house the greatest concentration of artists in Europe. Hang out in the "cool" new bars of Shoreditch and spot tomorrow's star, then move on to that haven of affluent bohemia, Notting Hill, to shadow entrepreneur Richard Branson, comedian Ruby Wax, writer Martin Amis or singer Annie Lennox.

Above: Richard Branson chooses to live in Holland Park, near Notting Hill

Creative Londoners

London has inspired the pens of thousands of writers over the centuries. Top areas for the more successful are the northern districts of Hampstead, Camden Town and Islington (chosen pre-*fatwa* by author Salman Rushdie, and by composer Michael Nyman and actress Cate Blanchett), reflecting a remarkable continuity with the past. Some houses have even been home to more than one famous inhabitant, as at 23 Fitzroy Road, Primrose Hill (Tube: Chalk Farm), once occupied by the Irish poet W. B. Yeats and later by the American poet Sylvia Plath. Plath was drawn to Yeats's blue plaque when on her way to visit her doctor and instantly decided that it was "the street and the house" for her. Within minutes of persuading some builders to let her in, she was at the agents, negotiating the lease for the top-floor apartment.

George Orwell (1903–50), in keeping with his sociopolitical concerns, lived closer to the pulse of less erudite streets, gravitating between Camden Town and rent-free rooms above a bookstore in South End Green where he worked. He later moved to 27 Canonbury Square in Islington (Tube: Highbury and Islington) – at the time a far from gentrified address. Another socially concerned writer, H. G. Wells (1866–1946), meanwhile lived in style overlooking Regent's Park from 13 Hanover Terrace (Tube: Baker Street). When negotiating the lease he said, "I'm looking for a house to die in." This he did ten years later, having survived the world war that he had so grimly predicted.

Chelsea has seen a stream of luminaries ever since Sir Thomas More built his stately house in Cheyne Walk in the 16th century, though this is now long gone. Exoticism and scandal always went hand in hand here, but Chelsea's notoriety really took off in Victorian times when custom-built artists' studios became the rage. At this time, Oscar Wilde (1854–1900) penned plays at 34 Tite Street (Tube: Sloane Square). Though Wilde's wife and children lived here, he was partying madly with his boyfriend "Bosie," a double life perfectly reflected in his novel *The Picture of Dorian Gray*.

Before the American John Singer Sargent (1856–1925) became London's most fashionable portraitist from his

Both T. S. Eliot and Ian Fleming (left), the creator of James Bond, were residents of exclusive Cheyne Row in Chelsea

souls and it was in Cheyne Row that Ian Fleming pounded out his first James Bond novel, *Casino Royale*, on a gold-plated typewriter while T. S. Eliot lived below. The latter's checkered marital life was exposed at 24 Russell Square in Bloomsbury, where for 40 years he worked for the publishers Faber & Faber (Tube: Russell Square). Literary hopefuls who mounted the steps often spotted Eliot's first wife, Vivienne, who would arrive wearing placards saying "I am the wife he abandoned."

Tite Street home, his compatriot James Whistler (1834–1903) was painting Chelsea's riverscapes from 96 Cheyne Walk. He was not the first, however, as the great landscape painter J. M. W. Turner (1775–1851) had already been inspired into abstraction from windows at No. 119.

In the 20th century Chelsea continued to attract creative

Money is now everything in Chelsea; gone are the bearded bohemians, royal mistresses and struggling actors, today replaced by the likes of former prime minister Margaret Thatcher (Chester Square), actress Joan Collins (Eaton Square), architect Sir Richard Rogers (Turks Row) and everyone's favorite foppish Englishman, actor Hugh Grant.

Actress Joan Collins has a home in Eaton Square

Blue plaques of Hampstead

John Keats (1795–1821), Wentworth Place, Keats Grove
Katherine Mansfield (1888–1923), 17 East Heath Road
D. H. Lawrence (1885–1930),1 Byron Villas
John Constable (1776–1837), 40 Well Walk
George Romney (1734–1802), Holly Bush Hill
Anna Pavlova (1885–1931), Ivy House, North End Road
Sigmund Freud (1856–1939), 20 Maresfield Gardens

Virginia Woolf, novelist and leading light of the Bloomsbury Group

Political exiles

With democracy stamped on the nation's soul and tolerance on its psyche, it is hardly surprising that numerous politicos on the run made London their base. Napoleon III (1808–73), Bonaparte's nephew, found himself exiled in London twice over and in 1848 lived at 1 King Street, in the gentlemanly heart of St. James's (Tube: Green Park). He became so inspired by the parks of the English capital that on his subsequent corona-tion as emperor he ordered his city architect to set about copying them in Paris. A century later, another Gallic exile, General Charles De Gaulle (1890–1970), was notoriously less of an anglophile, despite an equally salubrious address at 4 Carlton Gardens (Tube: Charing Cross). This was his base for organizing the Free French forces while broadcasting to resistance fighters before a triumphal return at liberation.

At the other end of the spectrum was Karl Marx (1818–83) who, after expulsion from Germany, settled in London to pursue a rocky, often impecunious existence. From 1851 to 1856 he lived in what was then a seedy Soho, at 28 Dean Street (Tube:

Tottenham Court Road), later writing much of *Das Kapital* in the British Museum's Reading Room. He was buried in Highgate Cemetery beneath a gigantic bust bearing the words "Workers of the World Unite."

Marx's wealthier compatriot, supporter and fellow thinker, Friedrich Engels (1820–95), was also buried in Highgate Cemetery after spending much of his life in London. From 1870 to 1892 he lived at 121 Regent's Park Road, a desirable address overlooking the park (Tube: Camden Town). Communist theoreticians continued to be inspired by no less a figure than Vladimir Ilyich Lenin (1870–1924), who in 1905 lived at 16 Percy Circus, near King's Cross (now the Royal Scott Hotel), within walking distance of the London Patriotic Society in Clerkenwell where he worked. This neoclassical 1737 building now houses the Marx Memorial Library (37a Clerken-well Green, Tube: Farringdon).

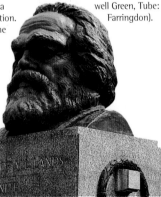

This stern image of Karl Marx tops his burial place in Highgate Cemetery

London's rural retreats

Visit London in winter and it looks colorless. Visit in summer and you'll be greeted by huge splashes of green, from perfectly manicured lawns to towering plane or lime trees lining streets and avenues. The great British love for all things rural is undeniable and the fact that the capital, despite rising pollution and traffic, manages to preserve this aspect must stem from some psychic feat of collective willpower. The squares of central London are bucolic havens carved out of the general mayhem. With a break in the clouds, Londoners are out there, on deckchairs, bikini-clad on the grass or striding across the parks.

Holland Park

One of London's prettiest and most secluded parks is a favorite getaway for residents of Kensington and Notting Hill. In 54 acres of grounds, wilderness and order are juxtaposed, although only the east wing of the Jacobean mansion survived a bomb in 1941. The park's intrinsic leafiness attracted a colony of wealthy artists to its fringes in Victorian days; these

Urban Green

included Frederic, Lord Leighton. His house, now a museum, includes an extraordinary arabesque hall and beautiful Pre-Raphaelite paintings. Today's well-heeled park *habitués* take in art exhibitions at the Ice House, lunch at the Orangery, or indulge in summer evening concerts in a tent on the lawn. Meanwhile, well-spoken families gather at the teahouse, squirrels, peacocks and rabbits roam in the woods of the northern half, and nannies and au pairs watch over their charges in the playground of the formal gardens. The Kyoto Japanese Garden offers a meditative retreat to the northwest of Holland House. Tube: Holland Park.

A statue of Lord Holland presides over the park to which he gave his name

desirable, white stuccoed residences within which lies the Inner Circle of botanical glories, with their fantastically diverse and fragrant rose gardens (including a Japanese-style waterfall, a favorite for Chinese wedding photos) and an open-air theater that optimistically stages Shakespeare productions on summer evenings. The open, northern section is where soccer players vie with the zoo's mountain goats for attention. On the western perimeter looms the copper dome of the London Central Mosque, and cosmopolitan strollers include Gulf Arabs, members of the orthodox Jewish community, and Chinese or Americans (the residence of the U.S. ambassador stands in the park). Tube: Regent's Park.

Islington Squares

The liberal intelligentsia of Islington's gentrified squares have been dubbed the "chattering classes," although they are now joined by bankers eager to live within spitting distance of the City. Unlike Kensington and Chelsea, the essentially Georgian and Regency squares of Islington are mainly public and surprisingly well-maintained, despite the regular onslaught of office workers' picnics, local children and, at times, the homeless. Southern Islington offers the

The Kyoto Japanese Garden in Holland Park

Regent's Park

The most northerly of the royal parks is the work of John Nash, "a thick squat dwarf with round head, snub nose and little eyes" (his own self-appraisal). Appearances aside, this visionary architect came up with the prototype for England's garden suburbs and cities, combining urban and rural in one fell swoop in order to lure the nobility to what was then considered far north of the fashionable West End. The 494-acre circular park is edged by the Outer Circle of highly

Parklife

In summer, the northern side of Hyde Park's Serpentine (➤ 130–131) sees Londoners out in force. Some picnic on the grass, but for the more energetic there is rollerblading or boating.

intimacy of Wilmington Square and its crumbling 1920s garden kiosk, the harmonious Palladian-style Lloyd Square (unusually private, because it is part of an estate) and vast, church-dominated Myddelton Square. Barnsbury, to the north, is home to elegant Gibson Square with its curious brick folly – in reality a ventilation shaft for the London Underground's Victoria line – and Milner Square, unique for its neoclassical architecture. In contrast are Lonsdale Square's unexpected gray-brick neo-Gothic houses. Tube: Angel.

Battersea Park

On 198 acres of land where the Duke of Wellington and Lord Winchelsea once fought an uneventful pistol duel (they both deliberately missed), Battersea Park was created in 1858. It catered to "tens of

Blooming mania

The Chelsea Flower Show takes place every year in late May and is traditionally part of the London social season. No other flower show can rival it in status.
The National Gardens Scheme organizes access to nearly 200 private gardens all over the capital. These are open at varying times between February and October. Information leaflets are available at tourist offices (▶ 35).

thousands of mechanics, little tradesmen, apprentices, and their wives and sweethearts." Today, its location directly across the river from Chelsea (earning Battersea the sobriquet "south Chelsea"), makes it an obvious escape for the people who live and work there, among others, interior decorators or antiques dealers from the King's Road musing on potential deals.

On the park's eastern edge loom the stacks of Battersea Power Station, closed since 1983 and now being redeveloped as a huge leisure complex. At the other end of the entertainment spectrum is the charming children's Zoo. The park's big surprise, however, is the Peace Pagoda, a two-tier building by the Thames erected in 1985 by Japanese Buddhists. Queenstown Road station

Left: The Buddhist Peace Pagoda in Battersea Park

Up the garden path

Less obvious gardens in London that are open to the public include:

Fenton House (Windmill Hill, Hampstead, tel: 020 7435 3471, Tube: Hampstead), a 17th-century house with a walled garden containing roses, an orchard and a vegetable garden.
Ham House (Ham, Richmond, tel: 020 8940 1950, Tube: Richmond), a Stuart mansion with formal gardens.
Roof Gardens (99 Kensington High St, W8, tel: 020 7937 7994, Tube: High Street Kensington). This is one of London's greatest bucolic gems, built in 1938 above a department store to be the largest of its kind in Europe and standing 98 feet above the high street. Three thematic gardens are Spanish (fountains), Tudor (red-brick structures) and English (streams, ducks and flamingos). It is now used as a private members' club and for functions, but entry is open to the public at other times.

COOL BRITANNIA

Suddenly, in 1997, it became cool to be British. Coinciding with a youthful, newly elected Labour government, a fresh face of the nation was propeled to fame from the galleries, studios, restaurants, clubs and stores of the capital. And today, although the catchphrase "Cool Britannia" is no longer so

Check out budding designers' clothes at markets such as Portobello (in stands under the overpass) and Camden Lock. Then cruise down Monmouth Street for emerging talent, and Bond Street and Brompton Cross for the big labels.

cool, still no other European capital can claim the same buzz, flair and above all hype that London generates as it rides high on a wave of prosperity and self-confidence. Fashion, art, architecture, design, music and film are the main ingredients of this heady mix.

It is not the first time that London has been swinging. The 1960s also saw a tidal wave of inventiveness, spearheaded by pop groups who did not necessarily originate in the capital but who just had to be there; The Beatles came from Liverpool, but their Abbey Road recording studios were the focus of the nation's music. London was the uncontested pulse of the nation with Carnaby Street, Kensington Market and the King's Road setting the tone for fashion victims, while Mary Quant, Biba, Ossie Clark or Mr. Freedom cut the patterns to match. Today, Carnaby Street may be a tacky tourist haunt with its own

Fashion from Vivienne Westwood (below)

The London Eye

The British Airways London Eye (➤ 104) has quickly become one of the city's landmarks. Londoners may initially have been wary about the prospect of a massive observation wheel, 443 feet in diameter, directly opposite the Houses of Parliament, but the superb structure, and the fantastic views from its capsules (below), are, in every sense, one of the capital's highlights.

Website and the King's Road is drifting into mainstream, but homegrown designers have matured into realism. Some, such as Alexander McQueen, John Galliano and Stella McCartney, even steer the fortunes of top couture houses in France, while London's grande dame, Vivienne Westwood, continues to stun. Above all, street fashion is still big. Even Parisian couturiers such as Jean-Paul Gaultier and Christian Lacroix admit to pillaging ideas from London's trendsetting young clubbers.

Facelifting

London's innovative architects are chiseling the capital's facelifted image. Architectural conservatism was the rule until the late 1980s, and included many misguided abominations, but great stylish swathes of glass and steel are now slotting into the city fabric. Many of these new buildings were designed by Sir Norman Foster and Sir Richard Rogers, originally partners in the 1960s before working separately on major projects in Europe and the Far East. Rogers' earliest landmark is the towering high-tech Lloyd's Building in the financial heart of London, which opened its doors in 1986, just before the yuppie bubble burst and recession set in. His latest contribution, and the capital's most controversial construction, is the Millennium Dome in Greenwich. In his turn, Foster, who in Hong Kong designed the headquarters of the Hong Kong &

Richard Rogers' Lloyd's Building

Shanghai Bank and the new airport, and in Berlin majestically rejuvenated the Reichstag, has created the Millennium Bridge, a much delayed result of decades of handwringing about the Thames. It is the first pedestrian bridge to be built over the river since 1900. Conceived as a purist "blade of light", the bridge connects Tate Modern with St. Paul's (though construction problems mean that it is not yet open to the public) and marks the general shift eastward of the city's cultural focus. In 1999, Foster was awarded the prestigious Pritzker architectural prize, so endowing him with true godfather status.

Another Millennium project, the much delayed and overbudget Underground Jubilee Line extension, is a showcase for architectural audacity with each station the work of a different designer, from

Best contemporary art galleries

The **Serpentine Gallery** (▶ 131), **Camden Arts Centre** (Arkwright Road, NW3, tel: 020 7435 2643) and the **Hayward** (▶ 110) show cutting-edge contemporary art. Private galleries vary from established dealers in and off Cork Street to the up-and-coming scattered all over Shoreditch and Whitechapel. Consistently showing significant British work is the **Lisson Gallery** (52–54 Bell Street, NW1, tel: 020 7724 2739, Tube: Edgware Road).

Foster at Canary Wharf, to Will Alsop at North Greenwich, Ian Ritchie at Bermondsey and the award-winning Chris Wilkinson at Stratford.

Art for art's sake

Provocative, sometimes scandalous, the Britpack (a convenient label for Britain's youngest generation of artists) is firmly anchored in the galleries and studios of the capital. Whether you love it or hate it, their work has become increas-ingly well known, particularly as star artist Damien Hirst has begun to broaden his interests, launching a number of popular restaurants and bars. Much of the impetus for London's most controversial artists came in the 1980s from advertising mogul Charles Saatchi who, in his large gallery space in St. John's Wood, continues to promote many of the artists whose work he collects. These include Hirst, the Chapman brothers and Gary Hume – all graduates of the University of London's Goldsmiths College, an institu-tion that has consequently attained near-legendary status.

Young designers

David Chipperfield, whose streamlined stores include Joseph on Sloane Avenue, and John Pawson, the much hyped king of minimalism, are among London's young design stars. Nicholas Grimshaw, whose soaring glass roof at Waterloo Station greets Eurostar passengers, is another designer to watch. Jonathan Ive's Apple iMac and James Dyson's innovative vacuum cleaner are recent megacommercial design successes; to see the work of more budding stars of tomorrow, pop into the Design Museum at Butler's Wharf (tel: 020 7940 8790. Tube: London Bridge ✛ 202 C2).

Maturer London-based artists include Rachel Whiteread, Anish Kapoor, Cornelia Parker, Richard Deacon and those doyens of East End-living, the double act of Gilbert and George, whose house in Fournier Street is a work of art in itself.

Far left: Spotted in all the right places – Damien Hirst, *enfant terrible* of the British art scene

Designer bars

Bars that reflect the capital's new aesthetics include **Pharmacy** (150 Notting Hill Gate, W11, Tube: Notting Hill Gate), **Alphabet Bar** (61–63 Beck Street, W1, Tube: Oxford Circus). **Denim** (4a Upper St. Martin's Lane, WC2, Tube: Leicester Square) and **Bank** (1 Kingsway, WC2, Tube: Covent Garden).

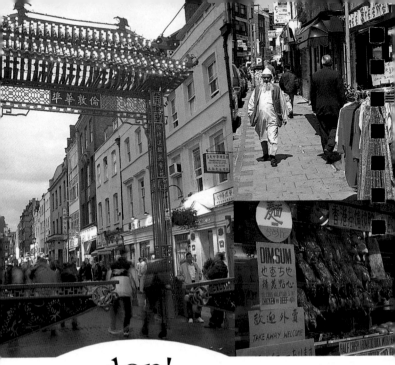

London's global
villages

The Tower of Babel? London's tapestry of cultures has had far-reaching influences on its character, its music, its literature, its streetlife and, not least, its eating habits. Ever since London's founders arrived in AD 43, namely the Roman army of Emperor Claudius, its citizens have descended from a variety of cultures, whether Angles, Saxons or Normans, all adding to a rich cosmopolitan flavor. Religious persecution later brought French Huguenots and members of the European Jewish community, while economic necessity brought Italians, Irish and Chinese. Large-scale immigration, however, really began after World War II, with a huge influx of people from newly independent Commonwealth countries. These new citizens became a much exploited low-paid workforce.

Today, inner city areas encapsulate a kaleidoscope of 37 different cultures, making up 20 percent of the population. Tension between communities has in the past exploded in street riots (Notting Hill in 1958, Whitechapel in the 1970s and

and politicians such as MP Oona King and Trevor Phillips, also a TV presenter.

The East End Jewish community has a lengthy list of rags-to-riches tales, whether hairdresser Vidal Sassoon or playwrights Harold Pinter and Steven Berkoff.

Whitechapel

Walking down Brick Lane, you'll hear the wail from the mosque or the beat of *bhangra* music, see traditionally dressed Bangladeshis, and smell the pungent aromas of a string of budget curry restaurants. The heart of this East End garment district, where street signs are written in Bengali, beats in the shadow of the Jamme Masjid, once a Huguenot church, in 1897 a synagogue and, since 1976, the Great Mosque, each reincarnation pointing to the dominant culture of the time. In 1700, London absorbed around 25,000 Huguenots escaping persecution in France,

Brixton in 1981). But as integration develops, it is increasingly difficult to separate the immigrants of yesteryear from those who were born and bred in London.

Young Middle-Easterners have an increasingly high profile in the music world, alongside more traditional roles in business, finance, law and restaurants. Just one example of a first-generation success story is that of millionaire Muquim Amed (born in 1963 in Bangladesh) who, starting from nothing in Brick Lane, now owns a chain of restaurants and is on first name terms with Prime Minister Tony Blair. Writers Salman Rushdie and Hanif Kureishi have also both imposed their global mark.

The African-Caribbean community has produced one of England's most popular news presenters, Trevor McDonald, as well as endless sportspeople, actors, musicians

London's streets reflect its ethnic diversity

Don't miss the 24-hour bagel shop, Beigel Bake, at the top of Brick Lane (No 159), an East End institution popular with taxi-drivers. The place is bustling at all times and on Sunday mornings, when Brick Lane's junk market is in full swing lines stretch down the street

A family affair – dressing up for the Notting Hill Carnival

and many set up silk-weaving businesses here, some with outlets in Petticoat Lane market. By the 1880s came another wave, this time from the Eastern European Jewish community who worked in the shoe and clothing industries. As they prospered and moved out, Bengalis replaced them to set up, in their turn, leather-clothes workshops.

Clerkenwell

Hip Clerkenwell, inner London's epicenter of loft lifestyles, is shaking off its history of crafts-people and immigrants. Huguenots, again, were the first, joined in the 19th century by Italians who peaked at around 10,000 between the world wars, living parallel to the Hasidic Jewish community, which still runs London's diamond trade from Hatton Garden. Although prosperity has scattered the Italian community, Little Italy preserves some trusty relics: grocery shops (Gazzano at 171 Farringdon Road for authentic customers and conversation), cafés (Carlo's at 7 St. John Street) and churches (St. Peter's is the official Italian Church, but the Holy

Opposite: Dancers at the Notting Hill Carnival

Redeemer in Exmouth Market truly echoes Italianate style) are steeped in Italian character and chatter.

Soho

Soho's Gerrard Street is London's Chinatown, lavishly announced by pagoda-style gateways and phone booths, at night joined by flashing neon ideograms. London's Chinese community dates back to the late 18th century, when East India Company ships bringing goods from the Far East disgorged sailors into the docklands. Some settled there to open stores, restaurants or opium dens, but it was after World War II that Chinese (mainly Cantonese) fleeing the Communist regime focused on the labyrinth of streets south of Shaftesbury Avenue. Few of London's 60,000 Chinese now live here but this area is the best window on Chinese culture. You can pick up that much-prized giant fruit, the stinking durian, a wok, a newspaper fresh off the presses of Bejing, an embroidered *cheong san* dress or devour a Peking duck in one of the many restaurants.

Notting Hill

The first group of 500 Caribbean immigrants shivered in the cold of Tilbury docks in 1948 but since then have made their exuberant presence felt. The Notting Hill Carnival (every August public holiday) is the zenith of Caribbean culture in Britain, with technicolor floats and costumes, throbbing reggae, steel bands, impromptu food-stands and cavorting crowds making it the world's second largest carnival after Rio de Janeiro. Ongoing gentrifica-tion is changing this area, however, and the unofficial clubs and relaxed cafés of the African–Caribbean community are slowly disappearing.

Chinese New Year

Chinese New Year is celebrated in true lion-dance style with fireworks, papier-mâché headgear, paper money and vociferous crowds. It takes place in late January or early February around Gerrard Street.

Wig & Pen

RESTAURANT OPEN TO NON-MEMBERS 12.30 P.

Two types of watering holes exemplify the often eccentric social traditions of London. By their very essence, gentlemen's clubs are reserved for the privileged few who pay annual dues to relax in the hushed atmosphere while traditionally perusing *The Times* over a Scotch. Pubs, meanwhile, are open to all comers, male and female alike, rich or poor, their often warm, smoky, jostling atmospheres a welcoming retreat for downing pints of beer while chatting to friends or strangers. On warmer days, customers at popular pubs will overflow on to the street.

Pubs & Clubs

Gentlemen's Clubs

There is no doubt about it, St. James's Street and Pall Mall are the epicenter of London's most distinguished and discreetly aging gentlemen's clubs. You won't be allowed in, but their stately facades betray just a hint of what goes on inside. These are the bastions of upper-class England where new members are admitted only on personal recommendation. Business deals, "old boy" networking, introductions and society gossip are the bottom line, while in the background a Reuters telex spews out the latest on City stocks and shares.

When first established as gambling dens, these clubs saw a string of scandals in the fine upper-class tradition of waywardness and eccentricity. Money was rarely a problem and vast amounts were lost or gained on the most trivial of bets – although in extreme cases this inspired bankruptcy and even suicide. At the oldest club, White's (1693), the diarist Horace Walpole recorded a typical incident: "A man dropped down dead at the door, was carried in and the club immediately made bets on whether he was dead or not." Brooks's and Boodle's were established soon after White's, setting a similar standard of excellence, and even today these three clubs remain top of the list for those in the upper echelons of British society.

Opposite: A taste for tradition – the Wig and Pen Club and Restaurant in Fleet Street

The RAC Club in Pall Mall

The Reform Club, founded by reformist Liberals in 1841, was a haunt of author Henry James and a hole was bored in the door of his favorite room so that the valet knew whether or not to disturb him. It was from the club's drawing room that Phileas Fogg, Jules Verne's

fictional hero, bet that he could travel around the world in just 80 days.

At the nearby Athenaeum, easily recognisable for its neo-Grecian frieze and dazzling gilt statue of Pallas, writers William Thackeray and Anthony Trollope both labored away in the library, while Charles Dickens was another pen-pushing member.

Members-only clubs continue to proliferate, above all in Soho, but the new generation is a far cry from its predecessors in St. James's. Women are accepted on an equal footing with men and it's the thirty-somethings who dominate. But the bottom line is the same: you are only allowed entry if signed in by a member. Today's most high-profile club is Groucho's, on Dean Street, home to the media and film *cognoscenti* who graduate from bar to restaurant.

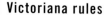

Since the 1970s, some clubs have relaxed the ban on women members although the Carlton Club, a bastion of the Conservative Party, had to make a special case to admit Margaret Thatcher. In others, women will be admitted as guests only or, as at the Athenaeum, only to a basement restaurant.

Victoriana rules

Many pubs still preserve the etched glass screens (known as snob screens), mirrors, tiles, wood paneling and lofty boarded ceilings of Victorian times. Track down these classics:

Red Lion
(2 Duke of York Street, SW1
Tube: St. James's Park, Green Park ✚ 197 E1)

Dog & Duck
(18 Bateman Street, W1
Tube: Tottenham Court Road ✚ 197 E2)

The Lamb
(94 Lamb's Conduit Street, WC1
Tube: Russell Square ✚ off map 200 B5)

Salisbury Tavern
(90 St. Martin's Lane, WC2
Tube: Leicester Square ✚ 200 A3)

Paxton's Head
(153 Knightsbridge, SW1
Tube: Knightsbridge ✚ 195 F2)

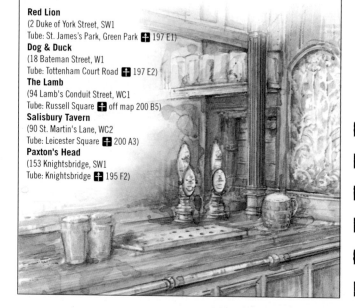

Pubs

Pubs are moving with the times, too. Some now produce cuisine that easily compares with top restaurants (see panel "Upgraded pubs") making for hazy distinctions between the two. Others have opted for satellite television on a big screen to boost pub crowds, with rousing atmospheres during major sporting events. But whatever the changes, pubs are still the mainstay for neighborhood or after-work socializing. They may have gone a long way from their origins, but the aim is the same – drinking and conversation.

It was the Victorian era that saw pubs multiply but in the more egalitarian late 20th century the classic division between unadorned "public bar" (where the serious drinking was done) and carpeted "saloon bar" (for couples and the middle social classes) has virtually vanished. Changes in licensing hours too have encouraged long afternoons that are spent continental-style at outdoor tables, and the cloistered atmosphere of Victorian times is fast disappearing.

Standards of comfort and decor vary wildly, as does pub food, but if you find the right one you may have the bonus of an upstairs fringe theater, art gallery or live music.

Traditional London pubs like the Dog and Duck are under threat from bland theme pubs

Pub etiquette

Pubs operate a system of first come, first served, so be prepared to elbow your way to the bar to order your drinks before sitting down. And remember closing is at 11 pm (10:30 pm on Sundays) – sometimes it's announced by "Time ladies and gentlemen please" and sometimes by the ringing of a bell. Beware of theme pubs and brewery chains: The true sense of a "free house" is that the pub sells beers from different breweries and the decor should reflect the landlord's and landlady's often idiosyncratic personal taste.

The Fitzroy Tavern

In its 1920s heyday, this pub on the corner of Charlotte Street and Windmill Street (Tube: Goodge Street ✚ 197 E3) had a heady history of disreputable local characters. Its queen, a fast-living character called Nina Hamnett, was immortalized by artists such as Modigliani and Gaudier-Breszka, befriended by Picasso and, as the saying goes, bedded by almost everyone else. Other permanent fixtures were artist Augustus John, resplendent in gypsy earrings and hat, and the poet Dylan Thomas, who fed his alcoholic addiction here.

Upgraded pubs

The Engineer (65 Gloucester Avenue, NW1, Tube: Camden Town) has a lively bar serving light meals and also a full-blown restaurant. A patio garden and mirrored upstairs rooms add to its charms.

Market Bar (240a Portobello Road, W11. Tube: Notting Hill Gate, Ladbroke Grove, ✚ off map 194 A4) draws the market crowds and local bohemia to its neo-Gothic bar and restaurant.

The Peasant (240 St. John Street, EC1. Tube: Angel, ✚ off map 201 E5), plumb in the middle of loft London, has a wonderful ornate bar with a tiled mural of St. George and a cool designer restaurant upstairs.

LONDON'S

BEST . . .

BEST FREE MUSIC
• In **Covent Garden's Piazza** (➤ 150–151) on a sunny day you'll hear anything from Vietnamese xylophones to Peruvian flutes or a homegrown electric guitar – or all at once.
• **The Barbican Centre** (➤ 88) on Sunday lunchtime holds free jazz concerts in the bar.

BEST BUS ROUTES
• **No. 7** – be spirited past the throngs of shoppers at Oxford Street department stores to reach Marble Arch, the Middle Eastern enclave of Edgware Road, Paddington station, hip Westbourne Grove and, through the backstreets of Notting Hill, end at Portobello Road.
• **No. 15** – cruise past the views from the shopping hub of Oxford Circus to Piccadilly Circus, Trafalgar Square, the Strand and Aldwych. Continue along Fleet Street, once the press

mecca, and up Ludgate Hill to St. Paul's, the Monument and the Tower of London (➤ 184–186).
• **No. 38** – enjoy a ride from Victoria through Belgravia, passing Buckingham Palace gardens, then along Piccadilly to Soho, the bookstores of Charing Cross Road and finally Bloomsbury – a few steps from the British Museum. Stay on longer for Clerkenwell and Islington.

BEST ANTIQUES AND JUNK MARKETS
• **Bermondsey Market** (Bermondsey Square, SE1, ✚ 202 B1) glitters with silver-ware, paintings, odd furniture and obsolete objects. Go at dawn on Friday to jostle with sharp-eyed professional antiques dealers for bargains.
• **Camden Markets** (➤ 152) is for anyone hankering after London street-style, crafts, jewelry, ethnic nick-nacks, design objects or furniture. Fight your way through teeming youth for fortification at countless drink and snack stands. Thursday to Sunday.
• **Portobello** (➤ 131) for anything and everything, from fruit and veg to specialist bric-a-brac, young designer fantasies or antiques – fake or sublimely real. Best Saturday.

BEST BRIDGE VIEWS
• **Albert Bridge** (Tube: Sloane Square). Not just another of Queen Victoria's odes to her

Top: The Oxo Tower Restaurant

Left: One of London's famous red buses

Above: Street performers in Covent Garden

Right: All that glitters... a stall in Portobello Road market

defunct husband, but a magically illuminated suspension bridge between Battersea Park and Chelsea. Take in views of the exclusive Chelsea Harbour development and Cheyne Walk to the north and monumental Battersea Power Station to the east.

• **Blackfriar's Bridge** (Tube: Blackfriars, ✚ 201 D3). The widest bridge on the Thames offers views of the expanding skyline of Southwark to the south – including Tate Modern, St. Paul's Cathedral and the spires, highrises in the City to the north, the South Bank Centre, Waterloo Bridge and Westminster to the west

• **Tower Bridge** (► 76–77). From this symbol of London you can see burgeoning waterside lofts replacing wharves as well as HMS *Belfast* on the south bank, and the dwarfed turrets and walls of the Tower of London alongside St. Katharine's Dock to the north. It opens for river traffic about 500 times a year.

If you only go to one...

...stand–up comedy show, head for the Comedy Store (► 66) with impromptu amateur acts or sets by polished professional comedians. Beware of hard-hitting audience participation.

...continental coffee–shop, indulge at Soho's Pâtisserie Valerie (► 158) or for loftier surroundings its offshoot on the second floor of art deco RIBA, 66 Portland Place, W1.

...bar with a view, hit the terrace of the Oxo Tower restaurant toward sunset (► 109).

For and against

London is the only place in which the child grows completely up into the man.
William Hazlitt (1778–1830)

London is a modern Babylon.
Benjamin Disraeli (1804–81)

Town life nourishes and perfects all the civilized elements in man. Shakespeare wrote nothing but doggerel verse before he came to London and never penned a line after he left.
Oscar Wilde (1854–1900)

London, that great cesspool into which all the loungers and idlers of the Empire are irresistibly drained.
Sir Arthur Conan Doyle (1859–1930)

Of course I got lost: for London is laid out as haphazardly as a warren. It is a myriad of Streets High and Low, of Courts and Cloisters and Crescents and full Circles, Paths and Parks and Parkways, and Yards, and Mews, and Quays, Palace and Castles and Mansions and Halls and mere Houses...there are Ways to go and Ends to be arrived at... London is, in other words, a maze, but I was simply amazed, surprised that it had taken me so long to realize I was lost.
Dale Peck, "Granta 65: London," 1999

I've learned to accept London as my muse. Initially, there I was, sitting on the tube, when she came in: filthy, raddled, smelly, old and drunk. But now we're inseparable, going round and round the Circle Line, arm in arm, perhaps for eternity.
Will Self, "Granta 65: London," 1999

I hate this daily ten-minute walk, along the outlines of the cold squares, past dark shopfronts where cats claw at the window panes, then into the tingling strip of Queensway, through shuddering traffic and the sweet smell of yesterday's trash.
Martin Amis "Success," 1978

London hates to let you go... If you drive out of London towards Brighton, there are seventy-five sets of traffic lights before you reach the motorway, and a dozen false dawns.
Ian Parker, "Granta 65: London," 1999

It is not a pleasant place; it is not agreable or cheerful or easy or exempt from reproach. It is only magnificent.
Henry James (1843–1916)

The vast town is always in movement night and day, wide as an ocean, with the grind and howl of machinery..., commercial adventure..., the Thames befouled, the atmosphere packed with coal dust; the superb parks and squares...the city with its vast moneybags.
Dostoevsky (1821–81)

A wet Sunday in London: shops closed, streets almost empty; the aspect of a vast and well-kept graveyard. The few people in this desert of squares and streets, hurrying beneath their umbrellas, look like unquiet ghosts; it is horrible.
Hippolyte Taine (1828–93)

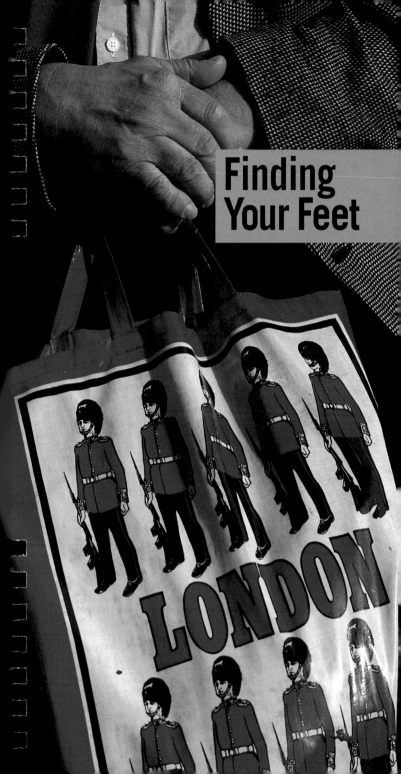

Finding
Your Feet

First Two Hours

Heathrow and Gatwick are the principal airports serving London. However, Stansted and London City Airport are increasingly busy with traffic from continental Europe.

From Heathrow
Heathrow (code LHR) lies 15 miles west of central London and is served by good road and rail connections. All the services below go from all four terminals and are well signposted.

- The **London Underground** (tel: 020 7222 1234), Piccadilly line, serves Heathrow from 4:58 am to 11:54 pm (Mon–Sat) and 5:57 am to 11:16 pm (Sun). The journey to central London takes about an hour and can get very crowded in the rush hour but is the most convenient, best-value option.
- The **Heathrow Express** (tel: 0845 600 1515) is a high-speed rail link to Paddington station. It runs from 5:10 am to 11:40 pm every 15 minutes and the journey takes 15 to 20 minutes – it's fast but expensive.
- There are two **Airbus Heathrow Shuttle** routes (tel: 020 7222 1234), each operating daily, usually every 30 minutes from 5:30 am to 9:45 pm. Buses make more than 20 stops along the way and trips typically take about 90 minutes to Victoria (longer to King's Cross). Heavy traffic can add considerably to this. No reservation is required. Buses are accessible for wheelchairs.
- Pick up a black metered **taxi** outside any terminal. Expect around an hour's journey time and £50 or more on the meter by the time you get to central London. Don't forget to allow for a 10 percent tip for the driver.

From Gatwick
Public transportation from Gatwick (code LGW), which lies 27 miles south of the city center, includes a 24-hour rail service.

- **Gatwick Express** (tel: 08705 301530) rail service runs to Victoria Station in central London. It is a 24-hour service, which runs every 15 minutes most of the day and hourly most of the night; journey time is 30–35 minutes. An alternative rail service is provided by Thameslink, which goes to King's Cross and Euston (tel: 020 7222 1234).
- **Gatwick Airbus** (tel: 08705 747777) operates every 60–90 minutes from 4:15 am to 9:15 pm to Victoria Coach Station. The journey takes up to 1 hour 30 minutes.
- **Taxis** operate from outside the terminal – journey time to central London is usually more than 1 hour 30 minutes and prices are around £80.

From Stansted
Stansted (code STN), small and modern, lies 35 miles northeast of the city center.

- **Stansted Skytrain** (tel: 0845 484950) to Liverpool Street station runs daily from 6 am until 11:59 pm and journeys take about 40 minutes.
- **Stansted Airbus** (tel: 08705 747777) to Victoria Coach Station operates 24 hours a day. The service runs every 30 minutes and takes around 1 hour 30 minutes.
- There's a **taxi** booking desk inside the terminal. Taxis into central London cost at least £60. The journey takes approximately 1 hour 30 minutes.

From London City Airport

London City Airport (code LCY) is the most central of the capital's airports, lying just 9 miles east of the city center.

- The best option is the **Airport Shuttle Bus** (tel: 020 7646 0088). Buses run to Liverpool Street station every 10 minutes Monday to Friday from 6:50 am to 9:10 pm, Saturday 6:50 am to 1:10 pm and Sunday 11 am to 9:10 pm. The journey takes 25 minutes and costs around £6 one way.
- Black metered **taxis** wait outside the terminal. The journey into Liverpool Street takes about 30 minutes and costs around £16. Expect to pay £20 upward for journeys to central London, depending on traffic.

Rail Arrivals

International rail services (Eurostar, tel: 08705 186186) from France (Lille and Paris) and Belgium (Brussels) arrive at Waterloo International Terminal where you connect with the Underground (subway) system.

Getting Around

Both London's subway system (the Underground or Tube as it is popularly known) and buses operate from roughly 5:30 am until just after midnight, after which a network of night buses operate until early morning. The system is divided into zones – six for the Underground and four for the bus system. These are marked on bus and Underground maps and displayed at stations. On both buses and the Underground you must have a ticket valid for the zone you are in or you are liable for an on-the-spot fine.

Travelcards and Bus Passes

If you are going to do a lot of traveling over a day or a week, buy a pass that gives you unlimited travel in that period. Make sure it covers all the zones you need – most of the places in the main part of this guide are in Zones 1 and 2.

- **Travelcards** are valid on buses, the Underground, the Docklands Light Railway and National Railways' services in the London area after 9:30 am during the week and any time on weekends or public holidays. **Weekend Travelcards** and **Family Travelcards** are also good value.
- If you need to travel before 9:30 am, then a **One Day LT Card** is available. All Travelcards can be purchased at Underground stations, London Travel Information Centres and National Railways' stations in the London area, or newsagents shops displaying a London Transport logo.
- For a weekly or monthly pass, you'll need a passport-size photograph.
- Reduced-price passes are available for children.

The Underground

The Underground (or Tube) is easy to use and good for longer journeys around the capital. The system operates on 12 lines, which are consistently color-coded on maps and signs. Once you know which line you need and the direction you'll be taking (north, south, east or west), follow signs to the relevant platform.

- Tickets and Travelcards can be purchased from machines or ticket offices in Underground stations.

- If you are going to make three or more Underground trips in one day, or a mix of bus and Underground trips, then **consider buying a Travelcard** (➤ 33).
- A **Carnet of 10** Zone 1 Underground tickets is a budget option if you will be making a number of trips in central London spread over several days. They are available from Zone 1 Underground stations or designated newsagents.

Buses
An extensive bus network operates in London. Though good for traveling short distances, buses tend to be slower on longer journeys.

- Some buses have a back entrance with no doors and a conductor to take fares; find a seat and pay when the conductor comes along.
- On buses with two sets of doors, you enter via the door at the front to pay the driver or show your pass and get off through the doors farther back.
- You need to know your destination and have change to pay for the fare.

Docklands Light Railway (DLR)
Docklands Light Railway is an above-ground rail system operating from Bank Underground station to Lewisham. Most visitors to London use it to get to Greenwich. For all ticketing purposes the DLR is part of London Underground, and Travelcards are valid on the DLR.

Taxis
Black cabs (many now painted in gaudy colors) are available from taxi ranks outside stations and hotels, but you can also hail them from the roadside.

- Cabs **available for hire** will have the yellow "For Hire" sign lit.
- All taxis are metered, and the fare will depend on journey time; there are surcharges in the evenings. Drivers expect a 10 percent tip.
- To ring for a taxi, **Radio Taxis** (tel: 020 7272 0272) and **Dial-a-Cab** (tel: 020 7253 5000) are both 24-hour services.
- **Black Taxi Tours of London** (tel: 020 7289 4371) offer a 2-hour tailor-made sightseeing tour.

Sightseeing Buses
Several companies operate private bus routes that cover the main tourist sights. The tour is usually in open-topped buses with a commentary in several languages. It's a hop-on, hop-off service, with stops throughout central London. For more information contact:
   Big Bus Company (tel: 020 7233 9533)
   London Pride Sightseeing (tel: 020 7520 2050)
   Original London Sightseeing Tour (tel: 020 8877 1722)

Car Rental
A car can be a liability in London; traffic is congested and parking expensive and elusive. Parking illegally can result in a parking ticket or having your car immobilized by a wheel clamp. It's only really worth renting a car for an excursion from the city. All the main international car rental companies have branches in central London.

Alamo (tel: 08705 993 000)	**Europcar** (tel: 0870 607 5000)
Avis (tel: 08705 900 500)	**Hertz** (tel: 08705 996 699)

Driving

To drive in the United Kingdom, you need a full driver's license or an International Driver's Permit (available from national motoring organizations in your own country).

- Traffic in the United Kingdom drives on the **left**.
- It is obligatory to wear **seat belts**.
- The **speed limit** in built-up areas is 30 mph; 60 mph on single carriageways; and 70 mph on divided highways and motorways (expressways).
- There are stringent laws against drinking and driving.
- Private cars are banned from **bus lanes** – watch out for signs informing you when they are in operation.

City Center Tourist Offices

London Tourist Board (LTB) runs the London Line recorded information system. This is a series of pre-recorded announcements (charged at premium call rate). Dial 09068 663344. A less expensive option is to visit the LTB's website www.londontown.com

Britain Visitor Centre
✉ 1 Regent Street
🕐 Mon–Fri 9–6:30
   Sat, Sun 10–4 (summer Sat 9–5)

Waterloo International
✉ Waterloo Station
🕐 Mon–Sat 8–6, Jun–Sep Mon–Sat
   8–7, Sun 8–6

Prices
The cost of admission for museums and places of interest mentioned in the text is indicated by the following price categories
Inexpensive – up to £4 (**Moderate** – £4–£7.50   **Expensive** – over £7.50

Accommodations

London is an expensive city and its hotels reflect this. The capital is simply too popular, and with not enough beds to go around, prices for hotel rooms are forced ever higher.

Hotels

The hotels listed below are the pick of the bunch: what they offer in terms of service, character, charm and standard of facilities is second to none. The **AA Hotel Booking Service** is a free, fast and easy way to find somewhere to stay in London; tel: 0870 5050505 email: accommodation@aabookings.com. Full listings of the hotels and B&Bs available through the service can be found and booked at the AA website: www.theAA.com/hotels.

Bed-and-Breakfasts

Bed-and-breakfasts (B&Bs) can be a less expensive alternative to hotels. At their simplest, B&Bs offer a room in a private house with a shared bathroom, but farther up the scale are rooms with private bathrooms in lovely old houses.

Budget Accommodations

For travelers on a budget, London can present something of a challenge.
- **Youth hostels** run by the Youth Hostel Association (YHA) are a good starting

point if you don't mind sleeping in bunks in a single-sex dormitory. You need to be a member of the Association and can join at any member hostel or at the **YHA Adventure Shop** (14 Southampton Street, WC2, tel: 020 7836 8541. Tube: Covent Garden), who will also supply a list of the nine London area hostels. Membership costs around £10 (£5 for under 18s).

- During the summer, usually from the end of June through mid-September, **university halls of residence** are let to non-students. These are slightly more expensive than youth hostels, but you get a single room (and there may even be a few doubles) with shared facilities. The **Imperial College of Science and Technology** (15 Prince's Gardens, SW7, tel: 020 7594 9494. Tube: South Kensington) is one of the best located, being close to South Kensington museums. **King's Campus Vacation Bureau** (552 Kings Road, SW10, tel: 020 7351 6011. Tube: Fulham Broadway) administers reservations for several centrally located King's College residence halls.

Seasonal Discounts

July, August and September are the capital's busiest months, though Easter and pre-Christmas are also popular periods, when room prices and availability are at a premium. In the winter months, especially November, January and February, rooms may be discounted. The period between Christmas and New Year is also relatively quiet (many hotels offer special rates after Boxing Day and before New Year's Eve – but you have to ask for them).

Prices
Prices are per night for a double room
$ under £75 $$ £75–£150 $$$ £150–250 $$$$ over £250

The Academy $$

This cozy, light, Bloomsbury hotel – not far from the British Museum – has been carved out of four Georgian townhouses. Bedrooms in particular have been thoroughly updated and are now fully air-conditioned; studio rooms are the most spacious and the best equipped. Food is good, too: The breakfast buffet is a cornucopia of fresh fruits, compotes, warm rolls and croissants, while the various lunch and dinner menus offer food with a Mediterranean slant.

🚩 197 E3 ✉ 17–21 Gower Street, WC1 ☎ 020 7631 4115; fax: 020 7636 3442; email: academyh@aol.com 🚇 Goodge Street

The Amsterdam Hotel $$

Although just a couple of minutes from Earl's Court Underground station, this stuccoed townhouse is set in a peaceful street. The hotel retains the house's original character while providing every modern comfort. Walls in the lobby and stairs are crowded with modern prints and a stylish use of pastel colors and fabrics distinguishes the 28 bedrooms. Guests have the use of a kitchenette.

🚩 off map 194 A1 ✉ 7 Trebovir Road, SW5 ☎ 020 7370 2814; fax: 020 7244 7608; email: reservations@amsterdam hotel.com 🚇 Earl's Court

Basil Street Hotel $$$

This hotel, whose location just behind Harrods could not be bettered, is one of the more characterful and old-fashioned London hotels. It wears a genteelly faded air, boosted by the charm of the ancient elevator, grand staircase and well-proportioned public rooms. Bedrooms vary in size and not all of them are *en suite*, but they are excellent value for money.

🚩 198 A4 ✉ Basil Street, SW3 ☎ 020 7581 3311; fax: 020 7581 3693; email: thebasil@aol.com 🚇 Knightsbridge

Bryanston Court $$

Look out for the smart blue awning that distinguishes this well-run hotel in a Georgian row not far from Marble Arch. The bar looks and feels like a gentlemen's club, with its leather chairs and old portraits; breakfast is served in the pretty basement restaurant where evening snacks are available during the week. Bedrooms are modern, but vary in size.

🔁 196 A2 ✉ 60 Great Cumberland Place, W1 ☎ 020 7262 3141; fax: 020 7262 7248l

Claridge's $$$$

Claridge's has, for over a century, enjoyed the patronage of visiting royalty, heads of state and dignitaries. A major refurbishment has brought the hotel's facilities right up to date, though outwardly little appears to have changed. Bedrooms now have the latest service systems and telecommunications, as well as a privacy button alongside those for maid, valet and floor waiter. Suites and deluxe rooms are outstanding.

🔁 196 C2 ✉ Brook Street, W1 ☎ 020 7629 8860; fax 020 7499 2210; email: info@claridges.co.uk 🚇 Bond Street

Five Sumner Place $$

Entering this Victorian townhouse feels like walking into someone's very smart home. The personal service is second to none and there are just a dozen bedrooms, all of which have a traditional feel and are well equipped. Breakfast is served in the huge airy conservatory, which doubles as a lounge. The South Kensington location is surprisingly quiet.

🔁 Off map 195 E1 ✉ 5 Sumner Place, SW7 ☎ 020 7584 7586; fax: 020 7823 9962; email: no.5@dial.pipex.com 🚇 South Kensington

Gate Hotel $$

The Georgian house is set in one of the trendiest streets in one of the most fashionable parts of the capital. Portobello Road antiques market (held on Saturdays) is on the doorstep. Although bedrooms are small, they lack for nothing, with a refrigerator, TV, radio, phone and shower room squeezed in. Continental breakfast only is served in the bedrooms.

🔁 194 A4 ✉ 6 Portobello Road, W11 ☎ 020 7221 0707; fax: 020 7221 9128; email: gatehotel@thegate.globalnet.co.uk 🚇 Notting Hill Gate

Goring Hotel $$$

One of the few top hotels in the capital to be independently run, the Goring is a wonderful example of a good old-fashioned British hotel and, as such, it is very popular. Guests are drawn by the blue-blooded appeal of the classic decor, the exemplary staff (many of whom have been there for years) and the excellent facilities, which run to fully air-conditioned bedrooms and power showers.

🔁 198 C3 ✉ Beeston Place, Grosvenor Gardens, SW1 ☎ 020 7396 9000; fax: 020 7834 4393; email: reception@goringhotel.co.uk 🚇 Victoria

Halcyon Hotel $$$

The Halcyon is an elegant townhouse on a grand scale offering a peaceful environment on smart Holland Park Avenue. The original Victorian character has been updated in a period style that mixes fine antiques and paintings with a light, modern color scheme. Bedrooms are spacious and well equipped with every conceivable extra. The restaurant is highly regarded, delivering some top-quality modern British cooking.

🔁 Off map 194 A3 ✉ 81 Holland Park, W11 ☎ 020 7727 7288; fax: 020 7229 8516; email: halcyon_hotel@compuserve.com 🚇 Holland Park

Hampstead Village Guesthouse $–$$

Antiques, bric-a-brac and family memorabilia clutter, albeit in a charming manner, this detached Victorian house just off Hampstead High Street. It may feel like a family home, but the facilities include all rooms *en suite*, welcome trays in every room and breakfast served in the garden (weather permitting).

Babies are catered to, including a baby-sitting service. Hampstead Underground station is just minutes away so it's handy for central London.

➕ Off map 197 D5 ✉ 2 Kemplay Road, NW3 ☎ 020 2435 8679; fax: 020 7794 0254; email: hvguesthouse@ dial.pipex.com 🚇 Hampstead

Hotel 167 $$

This well-kept small hotel, not far from Harrods and the South Kensington museums, has 19 bedrooms all with *en suite* bathrooms, mini-refrigerators and in-house video. Breakfast is served at a few tables in the charming lobby. The hotel's modest prices and good location make it essential to reserve well in advance.

➕ Off map 195 E1 ✉ 167 Old Brompton Road, SW5 ☎ 020 7373 3221; fax: 020 7373 3360 🚇 South Kensington

London County Hall Travel Inn Capital $$

This is one of several hotels in the Thames-side building that once housed the now defunct Greater London Council. It may not have the river views of the grander London Marriott County Hall (▶ below), but it scores points for its exemplary pricing policy (all rooms are a standard price). With neatly designed bedrooms and *en suite* bathrooms, it is one of the best deals for such a central location.

➕ 200 B2 ✉ County Hall, SE1 ☎ 020 7902 1600; fax: 020 7902 1619 🚇 Westminster

London Marriott County Hall $$$

The hotel, with spectacular views of the Houses of Parliament, Westminster Bridge and a broad sweep of the Thames, provides an excellent range of leisure facilities to accompany the well-laid-out bedrooms. It shares the vast site on the South Bank (formerly home to the Greater London Council) with London Aquarium (▶ 104).

➕ 200 B2 ✉ County Hall, SE1 ☎ 020 7928 5200; fax: 020 7928 5300 🚇 Westminster

The Ritz $$$$

César Ritz opened the hotel in 1906 following the success of the Hotel Ritz in Paris. It remains one of London's most fashionable hotels, distinguished by an exterior that is pure Parisian elegance and an interior that has been restored in *belle époque* style. French period furniture, colorful chintzes and gilt detailing to the molded-plaster walls, together with modern facilities like video recorders, provide exceptional levels of comfort in the bedrooms.

➕ 199 D5 ✉ 150 Piccadilly, WI ☎ 020 7493 8181; fax: 020 7493 2687; email: enquire @theritzhotel.co.uk 🚇 Green Park

Thanet Hotel $$

This family owned and run Georgian terrace house is right in the heart of Bloomsbury, with the British Museum a short walk away. The 16 bedrooms are pleasantly decorated and have *en suite* shower rooms. Back rooms are quieter. The price includes a full English breakfast, which is served in the cheerful breakfast room. Thanet Hotel is a tremendous value for money in an area not noted for good, individual places to stay.

➕ 197 D3 ✉ 8 Bedford Place, WC1 ☎ 020 7636 2869; fax: 020 7323 6676; email: thanetlon@aol.com 🚇 Russell Square

Vicarage Private Hotel $-$$

Situated in one of London's most exclusive areas, this hotel is a real bargain. The 18 bedrooms are a good size and the tall Victorian house retains a strong period feel and many original features. The down side, if there has to be one, is that only two of the bedrooms have *en suite* facilities, the others share the spotlessly maintained shower room and WC located on each floor. However, the price includes a traditional English breakfast.

➕ 194 B3 ✉ 10 Vicarage Gate, Kensington, W8 ☎ 020 7229 4030; fax: 020 7792 5989; email: reception@ londonvicaragehotel.co.uk 🚇 Kensington High Street

Food and Drink

London is regarded as one of the restaurant capitals of the world, boasting food styles and chefs from all corners of the globe, and finding a restaurant table in London on a Saturday night is no easy task.

New Trends

The explosion of new restaurants, even pubs, serving excellent food means that there is a wider choice of places to eat than ever before. Fusion cooking, incorporating ideas from all over the world, plus an entirely new school of modern Italian cooking, and the reworking of traditional British dishes into lighter modern cuisine have all made their mark. And to crown it all, some of the finest French cuisine to be found in the capital is being created by British chefs. For the food lover there has never been a better time to visit London.

Movers and Shakers

In the 1990s, two men from widely different backgrounds influenced the London dining scene more than anyone else. When, in 1989, the designer-cum-businessman Sir Terence Conran opened the Design Museum and adjoining Blue Print Café in a vacant riverside warehouse, few realized the impact this would have on the capital. It was a relatively modest opening for the trail-blazing Conran, who was already noted for the stylish **Bibendum** on the Fulham Road (► 132). From the amazing South Bank **Gastrodome**, which also includes **Le Pont de la Tour, Cantina del Ponte** (► 108) and **Butler's Wharf Chop House**, he has transformed dining habits in fashionable districts, first with mega-restaurants **Quaglino's** (► 64), **Mezzo** (► 157) and **Bluebird** (► 132) at the King's Road **Gastrodome**, and then with more controlled spaces such as **The Orrery** in Marylebone (► 157).

For a long time Marco Pierre White was considered the *enfant terrible* of the London restaurant scene. Arguably the best native-born chef in England, he still occupies pole position among London's star chefs, attracting success and controversy like a giant magnet – although he has now retired from the stove. He had grown into an astute businessman, scooping up prime sites and relaunching them stamped with his own exemplary style of complex modern British cooking. Two stand out: **The Oak Room** (► 63–64), in the Meridien Piccadilly, and the **Mirabelle** (► 63).

Up and Coming

With big bucks dominating the West End, the burgeoning restaurant scene has pushed out the boundaries of fashionable London. To check out the latest openings, look in the *Evening Standard* newspaper every Tuesday when formidable restaurant critic Fay Maschler digests the pick of the crop. Saturday and Sunday editions of *The Times* and *The Independent* newspapers also carry good reviews of restaurants, which are generally London based.

Be prepared to travel out of the center in search of the latest hit restaurant – the area around Smithfield meat market, for example, or Clerkenwell and Farringdon. These areas were once deserted after dark but are now booming, with stylish bars, stores and galleries jostling for the available space.

The Drinking Scene

Both Sir Terence Conran and Marco Pierre White can claim to have put the style back into drinking. The development of a new breed of mega-restaurants in the 1990s gave Londoners an alternative to ordinary pubs, where smoky, crowded conditions were often made worse by indifferent service.

One of the sharpest features of Conran's **Quaglino's** (➤ 64) and **Mezzo** (➤ 157), and Marco Pierre White's **Titanic** (➤ 64) are the smart American-style bars that attract some of London's coolest inhabitants. Popularity bred success, so much so that both **Bank** (➤ 156) and Oliver Peyton's acclaimed **Atlantic Bar & Grill** (➤ 62) made a real feature of their bars. Indeed, they have become so popular that they use vaguely intimidating door policies to retain an exclusive feel; the dress code is not strict and door policies do not apply if you have a reservation for dinner.

You can drink just about anything in these bars. Champagne, of course, is always a good choice, but all boast excellent wine lists, with many wines available by the glass and prices to suit all pockets. Bottled beers are classy European brands, and English real ales are often on tap – microbreweries produce their own beers; and hard liquor runs to quality brands not usually seen in pubs – Bombay Sapphire gin and East European vodkas, for example.

Budget Eating

In general, you would be lucky to get a decent meal and a glass of wine for less than £10 a head in London. But inexpensive eateries do exist. Pizza and pasta places can be good value, with the well-distributed **Pizza Express** group being the pick of the bunch as far as pizzerias are concerned. The **Pret-à-Manger** chain has captured Londoners' hearts with its self-service menu of fresh sandwiches, wraps, salads, pastries, and even sushi, made freshly each day from organic and non-genetically-modified ingredients.

Ethnic restaurants are also a good bet. If you head for Chinatown (➤ 159) there are many noodle bars and cafés serving inexpensive one-plate meals. Of the many Japanese restaurants in central London, an increasing number now offer great value set-lunch deals – there are no hidden extras if you stay away from alcohol. The South Indian restaurants in Drummond Street (Tube: Warren Street/Euston Square) are particularly good for vegetarians.

Afternoon Tea

Afternoon tea in a grand hotel is the ultimate treat. It's an excuse to dress up (nearly all the hotels listed here adhere to a jacket-and-tie code) and it costs less than lunch, but is often just as satisfying.

Prices
Expect to pay per person for full afternoon tea
$ under £15 $$ over £15

Brown's Hotel $–$$

Tea in the Drawing Room of Brown's Hotel is a cozy experience; it's like spending the afternoon in an English country house. There is a splendid Victoria sponge cake, as well as delicate sandwiches and fresh scones, jam and cream. If you indulge yourself in the whole tea be prepared to forgo dinner. Reservations are advisable, especially in summer.

➕ 197 D1 ✉ 33–4 Albemarle Street, W1 ☎ 020 7518 4108 ⏰ Daily 3–6 Ⓖ Green Park

The Dorchester $$

The Promenade, where tea is served, is soothing and luxurious, with deeply comfortable armchairs and thick carpets. A piano plays in the background and tea brings mouthwatering pâtisserie. Reservations are advisable.

➕ 198 B5 ✉ 54 Park Lane, W1 ☎ 020 7629 8888 ⏰ Daily 3–6 Ⓖ Hyde Park Corner

Meridien Waldorf $–$$

The Meridien Waldorf has a larger Palm Court than the Ritz, and probably the best setting for tea of all the hotels. It's like stepping back in time to the 1930s, especially if you go to the tea dance and celebrate with the set champagne tea. There's no formal dress code, but it is worth making the effort.

🚼 200 B4 ✉ Aldwych, WC2
☎ 020 7836 2400 ⏰ Mon–Fri 3–5:30; tea dance: Sat 2:30– 5:30, Sun 4–6:30 Ⓐ Covent Garden

The Ritz $$

The Palm Court, with its opulent Louis XVI decor, is the quintessential location for tea at the Ritz. This very touristy afternoon tea is expensive, but it remains an unforgettable experience. Reservations for either of the two sittings are required one month in advance (three months if you want to go on a weekend).

🚼 199 D5 ✉ Piccadilly, W1 ☎ 020 7493 8181 ⏰ Daily 2–6, reserved sittings at 3:30 and 5 Ⓐ Green Park

The Savoy $$

The Savoy is the most accessible of the capital's grand hotels, with tea served in the stately Thames Foyer. To the sound of a tinkling piano, an exquisite array of food is served, including miniature sandwiches, scones with jam and cream, and a selection of cakes and pastries.

🚼 200 B3 ✉ The Strand, WC2 ☎ 020 7836 4343 ⏰ Daily 3–5:30 Ⓐ Charing Cross, Embankment

Fish and Chips

Fish and chips (French fries) is the one dish tourists to London want to try most. Forget fusion, modern British cooking and the rest of the food revolution, here are four top-quality "chippies."

Prices
Expect to pay under £10 per person

Fish Central

Regarded by many as the capital's best fish-and-chip shop, there is also a restaurant where all manner of piscine delights are listed, from sea bass to sole. Make a reservation.

🚼 Off map 201 D5 ✉ King Square, 151 Central Street, EC1 ☎ 020 7253 4970 ⏰ Mon–Sat 11–2:30, 4:45–10:30 Ⓐ Angel, Old Street

North Sea Fish Restaurant

This is where the cabbies (taxi drivers) come. They usually occupy the back room, while the rest of the clientele sit in the front, among the pink velvet upholstery and stuffed fish. Portions are gigantic, and the fish is very fresh. Reservations are recommended for dinner, and there is a take-out service.

🚼 197 F5 ✉ 7–8 Leigh Street, WC1 ☎ 020 7387 5892 ⏰ Mon–Sat noon–2:30, 5:30–10:30. Closed Sun dinner Ⓐ Russell Square

Rock and Sole Plaice

This claims to be the oldest surviving chippie in London, opened in 1871. The Covent Garden location draws a pre-theater crowd to the restaurant and reservations are recommended for dinner. A take-out service is also available.

🚼 200 A4 ✉ 47 Endell Street, WC2 ☎ 020 7836 3785 ⏰ Daily 11:30–10, Sun 11:30–9 Ⓐ Covent Garden

Sea Shell

Sea Shell is probably the most famous of London's chippies. It is certainly very popular with visitors to the city – be prepared to stand in line as reservations are not taken for parties of fewer than six people.

🚼 Off map 195 F5 ✉ 49–51 Lisson Grove, NW1 ☎ 020 7224 9000 ⏰ Mon–Fri noon–2, 5:15–10:30, Sat noon–10:30, Sun noon–2:30. Closed Sun dinner Ⓐ Marylebone

Shopping

A vital wave of change has swept through the city's stores, and you will find an enthusiastic mood and glimpse a new modernism in London's shopping streets. Traditional institutions and long-established stores, however, continue to provide top-quality goods and deserve time on any visit.

Fashion

The capital's stores cater to a wide variety of tastes and pockets, whether you are looking for designer labels, a top-quality made-to-measure suit, or moderately priced high-street fashion.

- High street chain stores sell good quality clothes at moderate prices. **Oxford Street** (► 66), **Covent Garden** (► 159) and **Chelsea** and **Kensington** (► 134) have the best choice.
- Boutiques and smart department stores are the best bet for **designer names** and lovers of international designer labels will have fun finding their favorite names on either **Bond Street** (► 65) or **Sloane Street** (► 134).
- For those who favor a classical approach, **Burberry** has two outlets, one in Haymarket, the other in Regent Street. **Savile Row** (► 65), a shrine to pin-striped cloth and made-to-measure gentlemen's wear, also contains discreetly subversive tailors such as Ozwald Boateng.
- To find everything under one roof try the fashion-orientated department stores: **Harrods** (► 116), **Harvey Nichols** (► 134), **Liberty** (► 65) and **Selfridges** (► 66).

Art and Antiques

A thriving commercial art scene has both antiques and art from a time before Samuel Johnson's London, as well as pictures so fresh the paint is still drying. London caters to every visual taste.

- The **galleries of Mayfair**, primarily Cork Street and Bond Street, show established names and certain investments, with plenty of late 20th-century work.
- Many young artists have warehouse studios in the East End and a number of galleries here show exciting work at attractive prices. Listings magazines contain weekly updates of exhibitions and studio shows.
- If antiques are your passion the auction houses of **Sotheby's** on New Bond Street (Tube: Bond Street), **Christie's** in South Kensington (Tube: South Kensington) and, to a lesser extent, **Bonham's** in Chelsea (Tube: Knightsbridge) provide the best hunting grounds.
- The **King's Road** (► 135) in Chelsea and **Kensington Church Street** (► 134–135) are two long stretches of road lined by stores stuffed with furniture, ceramics, memorabilia and jewelry – eye-catching displays make for interesting window shopping.

Contemporary Furniture

Habitat, **Heal's** and **Conran** are still popular for furniture but are definitely resting on their design laurels; these days they are generally considered to be middle-of-the-road, disguised as modernist. Two stores selling furniture designs that are bang up-to-date are **Purves & Purves** (80–81 and 83 Tottenham Court Road, W1, tel: 020 7580 8223. Tube: Goodge Street) and **Viaduct** (1–10 Summers Street, EC1, tel: 020 7278 8456. Tube: Farringdon).

Specialist Food Stores

- The **Conran Shop** at Brompton Cross (Tube: South Kensington) and Conran's **Bluebird** in the King's Road (► 132) are terrific for stylish food purchases.
- Historic **Fortnum & Mason** (► 65) stocks a fabulous range of teas and a choice of 50 types of marmalade among other luxury foods.
- **Harrods** food hall, with its lush displays and own-brand comestibles, is irresistible to Londoners and tourists alike (► 116).

Markets

- Antiques hunters have to be at **Portobello Road market** (► 131) at the crack of dawn, but if you're hunting for clothes or are just plain curious you can afford to visit at a more leisurely hour.
- **Portobello** and **Camden markets** (► 152) are probably the two best markets for secondhand and unusual designer clothes, and just fun browsing.

Gift Ideas

Patum Peperium Gentlemen's Relish from Fortnum & Mason (► 65)
Luggage tags from Smythson's (► 134)
A classic silk tie with spots from Turnbull & Asser (► 65)
A silk scarf from Liberty (► 65)
Hologram cufflinks from Paul Smith (► 159)

Entertainment

The choice of entertainment in London is vast and listings magazines are invaluable for detailing what's on, whether it's theater, cinema, art exhibitions or gigs. *Time Out*, published every Tuesday, covers the whole spectrum of entertainment and is the best buy. Thursday editions of the *Evening Standard* (London's evening newspaper) and Saturday editions of national newspapers such as *The Times* and *The Independent* also have listings magazines.

Music

Diversity sums up the London music scene, and supports a serious claim to the title of music capital of Europe. Classical music is celebrated by five symphony orchestras as well as various smaller outfits, several first-rate concert halls, and high standards of performance. The ever-changing pop music culture that is the driving force behind London fashion and stylish restaurants and bars can feature more than a hundred gigs on a Saturday night alone, from pub bands to big rock venues.

- If you enjoy classical music, the **Proms**, an annual festival at the Royal Albert Hall, is held from mid-July through mid-September (► 136).
- In summer, informal **open-air concerts** are held at Kenwood House (tel: 020 7973 3427. Tube: Hampstead) and in Holland Park (► 13).
- The **Royal Opera** at Covent Garden (Floral Street, WC2, tel: 020 7304 4000. Tube: Covent Garden), stages elaborate productions with performances by the major stars. Alternatively, try the **English National Opera** (London Coliseum, St. Martin's Lane, WC2, tel: 020 7632 8300. Tube: Leicester Square), where works are sung in English.

Dance

Dance can mean anything from classical to flamenco and jazz tap, with London playing host to top international performers year-round.

- The **Royal Festival Hall** (► 110) at the South Bank Centre has an eclectic mix of dance programs, as does **Sadler's Wells** (tel: 020 7863 8000. Tube: Angel) in Islington, although it is better known for ballet. The **Royal Ballet** is based at the Royal Opera House, Covent Garden (Tube: Covent Garden).
- **Dance Umbrella**, an international festival of contemporary dance, is held at various venues around London during October and November (tel: 020 8741 5881 for information).

Theater

Theater in the capital is diverse, ranging from popular West End musicals to avant-garde productions in small fringe theaters.

- The **Royal National Theatre** (► 110) at the South Bank Centre (tel: 020 7452 3000. Tube: Waterloo) and **Barbican Centre** (► 88) produce all manner of drama. Also worth visiting is **Shakespeare's Globe** at Bankside (► 106). The **Royal Court** (► 136) and the **Old Vic** are the most dynamic theaters promoting the works of young unknowns as well as major new plays by avant-garde writers.
- "Off-West End" and fringe theater has a healthy reputation. The **Almeida** (Almeida Street, Box office tel: 020 7359 4404. Tube: Angel) and **Donmar Warehouse** (Earlham Street, Box office: 020 7369 1732. Tube: Covent Garden) are the major players, but theaters such as the **Gate** (11 Penbridge Street, tel: 020 7229 0706. Tube: Notting Hill) and **King's Head** (115 Upper Street, N1, tel: 020 7226 1916. Tube: Angel, Highbury and Islington) are also worth checking out.

Buying Tickets

The best way to buy a ticket for any London theater production is to contact the venue direct (so avoiding agency commissions). However, tickets for hit plays and musicals are hard to come by, particularly at short notice, and often are only obtainable through ticket agencies. **First Call** (tel: 0870 906 3700) and **TicketMaster** (tel: 0870 534 4444) are the most reliable. Credit card bookings made through these agencies are subject to a £2 booking fee.

- Buy your tickets directly from the concert or theater venue or from ticket agencies. **Never buy from ticket scalpers** – the practice is illegal and you may well end up with forgeries.
- If you are flexible about which production you want to see, try **tkts**, a reduced-price ticket booth at Leicester Square (► 160). Expect to stand in line and remember that tickets are limited to two pairs per person.
- The least expensive seats are always at the top of the theater, known as the "gods," but you will probably need binoculars.
- **Matinées** cost less than evening performances and tickets are far easier to come by.
- Some theaters offer **restricted-view seats** in the orchestra seats (stalls) at a reduced rate.

Movie Theaters

For movie-goers, The Odeon, Leicester Square, is recommended for the most modern and up-to-date movie experience the capital can offer.

St. James's, Mayfair and Piccadilly

Getting Your Bearings

The area between Buckingham Palace and Trafalgar Square is one of London's quintessential quarters, and if you have time for only a day in the city, you should consider spending it here.

A district of considerable wealth and architectural grandeur, this area contains the leafy squares and prestigious residential buildings of Mayfair, the exclusive gentlemen's clubs of St. James's, and the long-established stores and hotels of Piccadilly, one of London's great thoroughfares.

Previous page and above: Pomp and circumstance: the Horse Guards on parade

Here, too, is Buckingham Palace, the monarch's official residence, which since 1993 has thrown open its doors, in part at least, to the general public during most of August and September.

The area owes its original development to St. James's Palace, built by Henry VIII in the 1530s and subsequently the home of several later sovereigns, including Elizabeth I and Charles I (in our own time, the Prince of Wales moved here after his separation from Diana, Princess of Wales in 1992). The royal palace lent the area considerable social cachet, particularly after the 17th century, when King Charles II opened one of London's loveliest parks, St. James's Park, to the public for the first time. By the 18th century, members of the aristocracy who wished to be close to court had built fine mansions such as Spencer House. In time, sumptuous arcades and exclusive Piccadilly stores sprang up to serve the area's high-spending visitors and residents. In the 19th century Queen Victoria moved the court to Buckingham Palace, and the 20th century, saw the building of the present grand ceremonial route along The Mall between Buckingham Palace and Trafalgar Square.

Today, the area's elegance and refinement make it unique in the capital. You can enjoy the parks and grand walkways, the fine old houses, the stores and galleries (notably the Royal Academy, scene of major art exhibitions), and the principal sights at either end of The Mall: Buckingham Palace, with its famous ceremonial Changing of the Guard, and Trafalgar Square with the National Gallery, home to the country's premier art collection.

★ Don't Miss

At Your Leisure

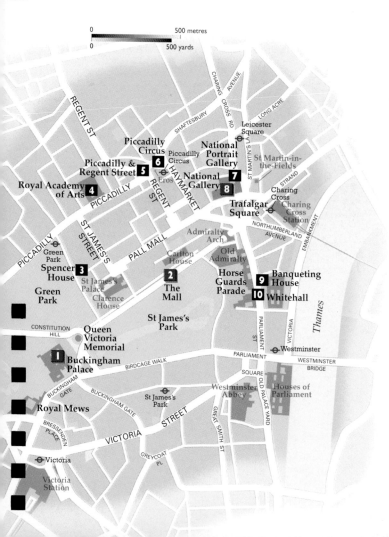

Enjoy a couple of royal palaces, some of the best-known sights of London, countless artistic masterpieces and the capital's prettiest park, right in the heart of the city.

St. James's, Mayfair and Piccadilly in a Day

One of the recommended highlights is the State Rooms in Buckingham Palace (▶ 50–51), but they're open only for around six weeks every year (mid-August through September) – and if you do visit them then it's unlikely you'll be able to

find a good vantage point afterward to watch the Changing of the Guard (or have the time to walk to Horse Guards Parade to see it there ▶ 53). Come back another day if you have your heart set on seeing the ceremony. You can still follow the plan below after visiting the palace, however – you'll just be doing everything a couple of hours later.

9:00 am

Start at ❶ **Buckingham Palace** (left, ▶ 50–51) – ogle the grand facade through the railings or, if you are here at the right time of year, visit the magnificent State Rooms. To avoid standing in line on the day see Top tips (▶ 51).

10:00 am

Stroll through **St. James's Park**, a tranquil oasis, and then walk along the broad, majestic, tree-lined ❷ **Mall** (▶ 52–53) to Horse Guards Parade to see the **Changing of the Guard**, one of London's most famous ceremonies. Be in place by 11 to 11:15 am to find a good vantage point.

12:15 pm

The Changing of the Guard over, walk through to ❸ **Trafalgar Square** (above right ▶ 53) for a close encounter with lions (statues) and pigeons (real). It's busy, noisy and surrounded by traffic, but it remains a natural meeting place, a national symbol of past glories, and an essential stop on any London visit.

1:00 pm

Time for lunch. St. Martin-in-the-Fields (above), next to the National Gallery on Trafalgar Square, has an inexpensive café in its crypt, and the gallery itself has a coffee shop and brasserie.

2:00 pm

Spend the afternoon seeing the gems of the superlative art collection at the **8 National Gallery** (▶ 54–57) – spend as long as you wish. If you're here on a Wednesday, the gallery doesn't close until 9 pm.

4:00 pm

Drop into the **7 National Portrait Gallery** (▶ 60–61) for a quick look at its appealing collection of portraits of famous Brits. Alternatively, make your way to **6 Piccadilly Circus** (▶ 60). From here it's a short stroll to some of Mayfair's squares and back lanes, or the **exclusive stores** of Piccadilly (right ▶ 58–59). You're also just around the corner from Leicester Square, the heart of Theatreland, with sleazy, flamboyant Soho and exotic Chinatown nearby (▶ 155).

❶ Buckingham Palace

The British sovereign's grandiose London home was built between 1701 and 1705 by the 1st Duke of Buckingham, but was redeveloped as a palace by King George IV in the 1820s, and became the official royal residence in the reign of Queen Victoria in 1837. Although it's a must-see for all visitors to London, at first glance it doesn't look terribly impressive – its stolid lines appear plain, solid and dependable rather than an exuberant celebration of majesty in stone.

While the palace isn't anything special from the outside, its interior is a different story altogether. The **State Rooms** were first opened to the public in 1993, a move prompted by changing attitudes within the Royal Family, and a desire to contribute funds toward the restoration of Windsor Castle (► 164–166). They shouldn't be missed if you're in London at the right time.

Above: The white marble Queen Victoria Memorial in front of the palace

➕ 199 D4 ☎ Inquiries 020 7839 1377; Recorded information 020 7799 2331; www.royal.gov.uk Credit card bookings: 020 7321 2233 🎟 Green Park ticket office, near the palace: Daily 9–4, Aug–Oct. State Rooms: Daily 9:30–4:15 (last entry), early Aug–Sep. Royal Mews: Mon–Thu noon–4, Oct–Jul; Mon–Thu 10:30–4:15, Aug–Sep 🚇 Green Park, St. James's Park, Victoria 🚌 Piccadilly 3, 8, 9, 14, 19, 22; Victoria Street 11, 24, 211; Grosvenor Place 2, 8, 16, 36, 38, 52, 73, 82 💷 Palace expensive; Mews moderate

Right: Buckingham Palace, The Mall, Queen Victoria Memorial and St. James's Park

The State Rooms are where the real work of royalty goes on, providing a stage for state entertaining, investitures, receptions and official banquets. Their sheer richness and decorative theatricality are mesmerizing, from the grand marble staircase and the brightly furnished drawing rooms to the Throne Room and the elaborate red-and-gilt State Dining Room. Your feet sink softly into plush red carpets, wall-coverings are almost works of art in themselves, and balustrades, doors, chandeliers and windows all display spellbinding and unforgettable detail. Equally compelling are the paintings that hang in the Picture Gallery, including works by Van Dyck, Rembrandt and Rubens, the classical sculptures and exquisite furniture. Check out in particular the thrones and the fabulously ornamental ceilings, which are some of the most elaborate imaginable. Don't expect to meet any of the Royal Family – they move elsewhere when the general public come to call.

BUCKINGHAM PALACE: INSIDE INFO

Top tips To avoid standing in line, **reserve tickets in advance** by credit card and collect them on the day from the Green Park ticket office. Arrangements can be made to have tickets sent out by post. Allow seven days for United Kingdom and two to three weeks for overseas addresses.

• Either buy an **official guide** (as nothing in the State Rooms is labeled) or rent an audio-guide.

• The **Changing of the Guard** ceremony (➤ 53) with bands and standard bearers takes place at 11:30 am in the palace forecourt and lasts 40 minutes. Get there by 11–11:15 am to get a good position – by the front railings between the gates is best.

In more detail Visit the **Royal Mews** to see the state carriages and coaches together with their horses. The collection's gem is the Gold State Coach.

• **The Queen's Gallery**, one of the finest private collections in the world, reopens in 2002 after a major refurbishment. Exhibitions change every six months or so. For opening times and prices tel: 020 7839 1377.

❷ The Mall to Trafalgar Square

The Mall is the grand, tree-lined processional avenue between Buckingham Palace and Trafalgar Square, a thoroughfare that comes into its own on ceremonial occasions such as the State Opening of Parliament and Trooping the Colour. Near the Mall are two royal parks: Green Park, which is at its best in spring when the daffodils are in flower, and St. James's Park, which is a delight at any time of year.

To start your exploration, turn your back on Buckingham Palace and cross the road to the **Queen Victoria Memorial**. This white marble statue, the Mall and Admiralty Arch were laid out in the early 20th century as a memorial to Queen Victoria who died in 1901. The statue depicts a rather dour-looking Victoria surrounded by figures representing the glories of the British Empire.

These days the Mall is a busy, traffic-filled thoroughfare, albeit one whose grandeur and dignity remain majestically intact. Until the 17th century, however, it was a small country lane, its confines used by King James I to play a French game known as *palle-maille* (anglicized to pell mell). A hybrid of golf and croquet, the game has long gone out of fashion, but it is remembered in the names of the Mall and Pall Mall, one of Piccadilly's main streets. Later, King Charles II improved the area, most notably by opening St. James's Park and Green Park to the public, a move that made this *the* fashionable spot in the capital to take a daily constitutional.

Above: Changing the Guard at Buckingham Palace

Right: The sweeping facade of Admiralty Arch

Top right: Nelson's Column dominates Trafalgar Square

Looking down the Mall on the left you can see 19th-century Clarence House, named after its first resident, the Duke of Clarence, who became King William IV in 1830. In 1953, when Queen Elizabeth II acceded to the throne, it became the London home of the Queen Mother. Behind Clarence House rise the red-brick Tudor turrets of St. James's Palace, built in the 1530s by Henry VIII (who died here). Since 1992, it has been home to Prince Charles, current heir to the throne.

From the Queen Victoria Memorial you may want to enter **St. James's Park**, following shady paths toward the lake; at the bridge you have a choice: One route takes you back to the Mall and a right turn past Carlton House Terrace, distinguished by its early 19th-century white stucco facade, leads you along the Mall to Admiralty Arch. Another allows you to continue along the lake to the far end of the park.

Either way, you should take in **Horse Guards**, the huge parade ground at the park's eastern end that provides the stage for the **Changing of the Guard** (► Inside Info, below). Then walk through Admiralty Arch to **Trafalgar Square**, laid out in 1820 as a memorial to British naval hero Admiral Horatio Nelson, who stands three times life-size on the 171-foot column at the square's heart. Reliefs at the column's base depict four of his greatest naval victories, of which Trafalgar against the French in 1805 – where Nelson died – was the most famous. The square's celebrated lion statues were added in the late 1860s.

The square's northern flank is dominated by the National Gallery (► 54–57), and – to its right – the fine spire of St. Martin-in-the-Fields, a lovely church famous for its concerts and with a first-rate café and brass-rubbing center.

TAKING A BREAK

Try **Chor Bizarre** (► 62) for an exciting range of Indian regional cooking, including a wide choice of vegetarian dishes and tandoori favorites.

THE MALL TO TRAFALGAR SQUARE: INSIDE INFO

Top tips The **Changing of the Guard**, where the mounted guards change over their duties, takes place in Horse Guards Parade, off Whitehall (Mon–Sat 11 am, Sun 10 am). The same ceremony for foot soldiers proceeds in the forecourt of Buckingham Palace (► 50–51). If the weather is bad, the ceremony may be canceled at short notice. (Daily 11:30, Apr–Jul; alternate days 11:30, Aug–Mar, tel: 0891 505452).
• If you have the chance, try to attend one of the **candlelit classical music concerts** held regularly in St. Martin-in-the-Fields. For information and credit card booking tel: 020 7839 8362 – the booking line is open Monday to Friday 10 am to 4 pm. Tickets are also available Monday to Saturday 10 am to 6 pm from the box office in the crypt. Free lunchtime concerts are given at 1:05 Monday, Tuesday and Friday.

8 National Gallery

The National Gallery has one of the world's greatest collections of paintings. Covering the years from around 1260 to 1900, it presents the cream of the nation's art collection, including some 2,200 works of European art hung in a succession of light, well-proportioned rooms. Pick a famous painter from almost any era – Botticelli, Canaletto, Cézanne, Constable, Leonardo da Vinci, Monet, Rembrandt, Renoir, Raphael, Titian, Turner, Van Gogh – and the chances are they'll be represented here.

Suggested Route

The gallery is divided into **four wings**, each covering a chronological period: it makes sense to visit the wings in this order:

- **Sainsbury Wing** 1260 to 1510 Rooms 51–66
- **West Wing** 1510 to 1600 Rooms 2–12
- **North Wing** 1600 to 1700 Rooms 14–32
- **East Wing** 1700 to 1900 Rooms 33–46

The National Gallery was designed as the architectural focus of Trafalgar Square

🞣 197 F1
✉ Trafalgar Square, WC2
☎ 020 7747 2885;
www.nationalgallery.org.uk
🕑 Daily 10–6 (Wed 10–9); The Micro Gallery: daily

10–5:30 (Wed 10–8:30). Closed Jan 1, Good Friday and Dec 24–26
🚇 Charing Cross, Leicester Square
🚌 3, 6, 9, 11, 12, 13, 15, 23, 24, 29, 53, 77A, 88, 91, 139, 159, 176
🎫 Free

An allegory of motherhood – the celebrated Leonardo da Vinci cartoon in the National Gallery depicts the Madonna and Child with a young John the Baptist and St. Anne, the mother of the Virgin Mary

Sainsbury Wing

The wonderfully airy Sainsbury Wing (named after the supermarket dynasty that sponsored it) was designed by architect Robert Venturi and opened in 1991. Although it is the newest part of the gallery, it displays the oldest paintings, in particular the masterpieces of the various Italian schools after about 1300. Two of its loveliest works are by Leonardo da Vinci (Room 51). The unfinished *The Virgin of the Rock* (1508) depicts Mary, John the Baptist and Christ with an angel in a rocky landscape. Some of the work may be by pupils, but the sublime expression on the angel's face suggests pure Leonardo. In a specially darkened room nearby, da Vinci's cartoon of *The Virgin and Child with St. Anne and St. John the Baptist* (1508) is an exquisitely beautiful depiction of a meeting never mentioned in the Bible – Christ and his maternal grandmother.

Be certain to see *The Wilton Diptych* (Room 53), a late 14th-century altarpiece commissioned by Richard II for his private prayers: It shows the King kneeling on the left and being presented to the Madonna and Child. Both the artist and his nationality remain a mystery. Less tantalizing but no less beautiful are two portraits, Van Eyck's *Arnolfini Portrait* (Room 56) and Giovanni Bellini's matchless *Doge Leonardo Loredan* (Room 61).

West Wing

Turn around as you cross from the Sainsbury to the West Wing for the gallery's most remarkable view – a series of receding archways designed to frame a Renaissance altarpiece on a distant wall. In the West Wing are mostly French, Italian and Dutch works from the High Renaissance. Perhaps the most memorable is Hans Holbein the Younger's *The Ambassadors* (1533) – almost life-size portraits of Jean de Dinteville and Georges de Selve (Room 4). The picture is crammed with symbol and allusion, mostly aimed at underlining the fleeting nature of earthly life. In the middle foreground of the picture is a clever *trompe l'oeil* of what appears face on to be simply a white disc; move to the right side of the painting (foot marks on the floor indicate the correct position), and it's revealed as a human skull.

North Wing

Painters who challenged the primacy of the Italians during the 16th and 17th centuries are the stars of the North Wing – Rubens, Rembrandt, Van Dyck, Velázquez, Vermeer and Claude, to name but a handful. Velázquez's *The Toilet of Venus* (also known as *The Rokeby Venus* after Rokeby Hall where it once hung) is one of the best-known paintings (Room 29). It is an unusual work, firstly because it shows a back view of the goddess (with an extraordinary face captured in a mirror), and secondly because it is a nude, a genre frowned upon by the Inquisition in Spain when the work was completed in 1651.

East Wing

The East Wing is often the busiest in the gallery, mainly because it contains some of the best-known of all British paintings. Chief among these is John Constable's *The Hay Wain* (Room 34), first exhibited in 1821 when the fashion was for blended brushwork and smooth painted texture: Contemporary critics disapproved of what they saw as the painting's rough and unfinished nature. Today it represents an archetype of an all-but-vanished English rural landscape. More works by Constable are on display in Tate Britain (➤ 102) and the Victoria and Albert Museum (➤ 117–120).

J. M. W. Turner, though a contemporary of Constable, developed a radically different style. In his day he was considered madly eccentric, particularly in his later works, yet it is these mature paintings that have the most profound modern-day resonance. Two of the greatest, *The Fighting Téméraire* (1838) and *Rain, Steam and Speed* (1844), display the powerful and almost hallucinatory effects of light on air and water characteristic of the painter (Room 34). More of the same can be seen in Tate Britain's Clore Gallery (➤ 102).

Equally as popular as the Turners and Constables are the National's numerous Impressionist masterpieces (Rooms 43 and 46), including a wealth of instantly recognizable paintings such as Van Gogh's *Sunflowers* (1889) and Seurat's *The Bathers at Asnières* (1884), the latter's shimmering clarity a fitting memory to take with you back into Trafalgar Square.

TAKING A BREAK

You can get light refreshments at **Crivelli's Garden** (➤ 62), in the Sainsbury Wing of the gallery.

The splendid interior of the National Gallery provides a suitably grand setting for one of the greatest collections of paintings in Europe

The Bathers at Asnières by Georges Seurat is among the best known of the National Gallery's many Impressionist masterpieces

NATIONAL GALLERY: INSIDE INFO

Top tips The gallery displays many British artists, but many more, especially modern British painters, are better represented in Tate Britain's collection (➤ 102).
• **Soundtrack** is an excellent portable CD guide. It covers the entire collection – simply dial up the number beside the picture to hear a commentary. Although this is in English, there is a highlights tour of 30 major works that is available in six languages. It's free, but a donation is requested.

In more detail The **Micro Gallery** in the Sainsbury Wing contains a computerized information system with information on every painting and artist in the collection.

Hidden gem Most of the pictures owned by the National Gallery are on display – those not in the main galleries are in the **lower floor galleries** in the main building. Telephone before visiting to make sure that these lower galleries are open; they are closed when staffing levels are low.

At Your Leisure

3 Spencer House

Spencer House is London's finest surviving 18th-century townhouse and one of the capital's best-kept secrets. Excellent hour-long guided tours provide background information on the house, its painstaking ten-year restoration and its original incumbents, the Spencer family, the most famous member of which was Lady Diana Spencer, later Diana, Princess of Wales (1961–97).

The house was built for the first Earl Spencer and his wife, Georgiana, who desired a London home to complement their country seat at Althorp in Northamptonshire. Virtually all of the decoration (cherubs, roses, palms and turtle doves) celebrates the pair's love for one another. The painted ceilings, walls, friezes and gilded ornamentation are breathtaking throughout.

The Dining Room and Great Room are large and grand, and book-lovers will long for a few private hours in the Library with its towering wooden bookcases and leather-bound books. Most visitors enjoy the Palm Room, where each column is covered with elaborately carved and gilded palm fronds (the furniture has a matching motif).

➕ 199 D5
✉ 27 St. James's Place, SW1 ☎ 020 7514 1964
🕐 Sun 10:30– 5:45, Feb–Jul and Sep–Dec. Last tour 4:45. Children aged under 10 not admitted
🍴 Cafés and restaurants along Piccadilly
🚇 Green Park
🚌 8, 9, 14, 19, 22, 38
💷 Moderate

4 Royal Academy of Arts

Burlington House is one of the few remaining 18th-century Piccadilly mansions. Today it houses one of London's most illustrious art galleries, the Royal Academy, which stages a variety of high-profile exhibitions. June through August sees its annual Summer Exhibition, for which every aspiring artist in the country hopes to have a piece selected.

➕ 197 D1 ✉ Burlington House, Piccadilly, W1 ☎ 020 7300 8000; www.royalacademy.org.uk 🕐 Daily 10–6 (Fri 10–8:30) 🍴 Café and restaurant 🚇 Piccadilly Circus, Green Park 🚌 9, 14, 19, 22, 38 💷 Admission charge depends on the exhibition

5 Piccadilly and Regent Street shopping

If you need a change from sightseeing, take time off to visit some of London's most exclusive stores: Piccadilly, St. James's and Regent Street (► 65–66) are home to some of London's finest stores.

The best of the Piccadilly stores are the old-fashioned book-store,

Hatchards, the high-class grocery turned department store, **Fortnum & Mason** (▶ 65), and the covered arcades of prestigious stores that lead off to left and right. **Burlington Arcade**, where top-hatted beadles ensure shoppers act with due decorum (there are regulations against singing and hurrying), is the best known. Piccadilly itself was named in honor of a 17th-century tailor who made his fortune from collars known as "picadils." The mansion he built became known as Piccadilly Hall, in time lending its name to the entire street. These days much of the tailoring has moved north of Piccadilly to

Savile Row and south to **Jermyn Street** (▶ 65).

Liberty in Regent Street is a department store of class and character, with plush carpets, wood paneling and a balconied hall hung with glorious fabrics (▶ 65).

✚ 197 E1

Piccadilly and Regent Street are home to exclusive stores such as Fortnum & Mason (above), famed for its sumptuous food, and Liberty, whose interior (right) is an Aladdin's Cave of luxury goods. At elegant Burlington Arcade, beadles (top right) enforce regulations against singing and hurrying

Regent Street is one of the capital's premier shopping streets

introduced in the early 20th century, and have become something of a London icon – come after dark for the best effects.

For all its faults, the Circus is useful as a jumping-off point to other sights; along Shaftesbury Avenue toward Chinatown or Soho, along Coventry Street to Leicester Square, or to Regent Street and Piccadilly.
✚ 197 E1

⑦ National Portrait Gallery

The gallery houses a fascinating and strangely beguiling collection of paintings, sculptures and photographs of eminent Britons past and present. The material dates from the early 16th century to the modern era, and includes many of the country's most famous faces. Whatever your fields of interest, you'll almost certainly find something here to interest you.

The monarchs represented include Richard III, Henry VII, Henry VIII, Elizabeth I (depicted several times) and many members of the present Royal Family. However, it is the portraits of commoners that are most memorable. There is a supposed portrait of Shakespeare, a drawing of Jane Austen by her sister, the Brontë sisters by their brother Patrick and striking photographs of Oscar Wilde, Virginia Woolf and Alfred, Lord Tennyson.

⑥ Piccadilly Circus

While Piccadilly Circus features large in the minds of visitors to the city (a photograph in front of the statue at its heart is almost obligatory), most Londoners dismiss it as a tacky melee of tourists, traffic and noise.

The Eros statue, which actually represents the Angel of Christian Charity not the Greek god of love, was erected in 1893 to commemorate Antony Cooper, 7th Earl of Shaftesbury (1801–85), a tireless campaigner for workers, the poor and the mentally ill. The neon advertisements were

Eros and the bright lights of Piccadilly Circus are best seen at night

Among recent literary stars are Salman Rushdie and Dame Iris Murdoch.

Politicians and figures from the arts, sciences, sport and media are also well represented. Look for the portraits of British prime ministers Margaret Thatcher and Harold Wilson, scientist Stephen Hawking, film director Alfred Hitchcock and soccer player Bobby Charlton.

➕ 197 F1 ✉ St. Martin's Place, WC2 ☎ 020 7306 0055; www.npg.org.uk ⏰ Mon–Sat 10–6, Sun noon–6; closed Jan 1, Good Friday, May Day public holiday and Dec 24–26 🚇 Charing Cross, Leicester Square 🍽 Café in the basement 🚌 3, 6, 9, 11, 12, 13, 15, 23, 24, 29, 53, 77A, 88, 91, 139, 159, 176 💳 Admission free (charge for some exhibitions)

🄉 Banqueting House

The Banqueting House is the only remaining part of the old Palace of Whitehall, formerly the monarch's official home, which was destroyed by fire in 1698. It was built by the great architect Inigo Jones in the early 17th century, and includes a painted ceiling by Flemish artist Peter Paul Rubens as its decorative centerpiece. The ceiling was commissioned in 1635 by the king, Charles I, who paid the artist $4,300, an astronomical sum at that time. This, and other paintings were all conceived as paeans to Charles's father, James I.

It was from a window of the Banqueting House that, on January 30, 1649, Charles I, tried and convicted of high treason following the defeat of Royalist forces in the English Civil War, stepped on to the scaffold and faced his executioner. As he went to his death, branded an enemy of state, he remarked, "I have a good cause and a gracious God on my side."

➕ 200 A2 ✉ Whitehall ☎ 020 7930 4179; www.hrp.org.uk ⏰ Mon–Sat 10–5; closed public holidays, and for special functions 🚇 Westminster, Charing Cross 🚌 3, 11, 12, 24, 53, 77A, 88, 159 💳 Inexpensive; audio guide included

🄊 Whitehall

This busy, but undistinguished, street lined by the bland facades of government offices takes you south from Trafalgar Square through the heart of British Government. Downing Street, a side turning blocked off by a large gate, is where the British prime minister has his (or her) official residence. Traditionally this is at No. 10, while No. 11 plays host to the Chancellor of the Exchequer, though the present prime minister Tony Blair and his family reside at the larger No. 11. The only real patch of color is provided by the mounted soldiers at Horse Guards.

At the center of Whitehall is the Cenotaph, a memorial to the war dead and the solemn focus of the annual Remembrance Day Ceremony in November.

➕ 200 A2

For Kids

• The colorful Changing of the Guard ceremony at Buckingham Palace and/or Horse Guards (▶ 51).

• A visit to Hamleys toy shop (▶ 65) and the Disney Store, both in Regent Street.

• Feeding the ducks in St. James's Park (▶ 53).

Where to...
Eat and Drink

Prices

Expect to pay per person for a meal excluding drinks and service
$** under £25   **$$** £25–£50   **$$$ over £50

Atlantic Bar & Grill $$

Sweep down the grand staircase into a noisy, dramatically lit cavernous space, filled with a cosmopolitan crowd. Some are here just for a drink at the clamorous bar, but the food is worth investigation. There's a slight Mediterranean-cum-oriental twist to the whole menu, but the classics are equally pleasing. Dinner reservations are essential. Smart dress is required.

+ **197 E1** ⊠ **20 Glasshouse Street, W1** ☎ **020 7734 4888; fax: 020 7734 3609** ⊕ **Lunch: Mon–Fri noon–2:45. Dinner: Mon–Sat 6–11:30, Sun 7–10:30** Ⓜ **Piccadilly Circus**

Le Caprice $$–$$$

This famous restaurant, tucked neatly behind the Ritz hotel, attracts a smart celebrity crowd. Despite the stark white walls and black-and-chrome furniture, the atmosphere is far from intimidating, and the fast-paced service remains friendly at all times. The menu is a great mix of classic brasserie dishes balanced by some more lively up-to-date ideas.

+ **199 D5** ⊠ **Arlington Street, SW1** ☎ **020 7629 2239; fax: 020 7493 9040** ⊕ **Lunch: Mon–Sat noon–3, Sun noon–4. Dinner: Mon–Sat 5:30–midnight, Sun 6–midnight** Ⓜ **Green Park**

Chor Bizarre $$

This overseas branch of the New Delhi restaurant embraces its name (which means "thieves' market") with gusto, displaying a crowded and exotic collection of Indian antiques and artifacts. The menu explores the regions of India with some imagination, and provides a good choice of vegetarian dishes and tandoori favorites. Wines have been carefully chosen to complement the food.

+ **197 D1** ⊠ **16 Albemarle Street, W1** ☎ **020 7629 9802/7629 8542; fax: 020 7493 7756** ⊕ **Mon–Sat noon–3, 6–11:30. Sun noon–2:30, 6–10:30** Ⓜ **Green Park**

Crivelli's Garden $–$$

Climb the wide, stone staircase of the National Gallery's Sainsbury Wing, take a sharp left turn, and enter what appears to be an upscale bar and cafeteria. In the bar, there's a good choice of snacks, including bruschetta and panini, each with a recommended glass of wine, plus salads and pizza. In the restaurant, the menu provides a mixture of Provencale and northern Italian cooking. You can choose from a good selection of wines by the glass, as well as moderately priced bottles of wine.

+ **197 F1** ⊠ **The National Gallery, WC2** ☎ **020 7747 2869; fax: 020 7747 2438** ⊕ **Mon, Tue, Thu–Sun 10–5, Wed 10–8** Ⓜ **Charing Cross**

Le Gavroche $$$

Le Gavroche, London's longest-running French restaurant, is comfortable rather than opulent, with tables that are generous in size and service that is smoothly, soothingly efficient. For many years Albert Roux's classic French cooking was the solid rock on which the restaurant's seasonally changing menus were built, but now that son Michel has taken over, ideas, although firmly rooted in that same classic tradition, have moved with the times. The cooking is still confident and skilled, but with a lighter touch. The wine list is aristocratic, with prices to match.

🏠 196 B1 ✉ 43 Upper Brook Street, W1 ☎ 020 7408 0881/7499 1826; fax: 020 7409 0939/7491 4387 🕐 Mon–Fri noon–2, 7–11 🚇 Marble Arch

La Madeleine $

This truly French cafe lies just off Regent Street. Kick-start the day with a buttery croissant and make a light lunch of a *croque monsieur* or a range of salads. At any time of the day a vast array of tarts, pastries and all sorts of cream-filled delights will be appropriate. The staff are charming and there is limited seating on the sidewalk outside.

🏠 197 D1 ✉ 5 Vigo Street, W1 ☎ 020 7734 8353 🕐 Mon–Sat 8–8, Sun 11–7 🚇 Green Park, Piccadilly

Mirabelle $$-$$$

Rescued from oblivion by chef Marco Pierre White, the Mirabelle has reemerged as one of the most fashionable places to eat in London, serving MPW's trademark first-class classic French-style cooking. The restaurant's revamped decor matches an easier, less formal style, though tables are perhaps a little too close together. Lunch is especially good value, with the keenly priced menu ensuring that the place is packed. Get a reservation for a patio table in good weather.

🏠 198 C5 ✉ 56 Curzon Street, W1 ☎ 020 7499 4636; fax: 020 7499 5449 🕐 Lunch: Mon–Sat noon–2.30, Sun 1–3. Dinner: Mon–Sat 6–11.30, Sun 6–10.30 🚇 Green Park

Mitsukoshi $$

This smart, comfortable restaurant is located on the lower first floor of a Japanese department store. The a la carte selection includes classic Japanese dishes, but choosing one of the many set meals will give an excellent introduction to the cuisine. These range from a simple *hana*, which includes an appetizer, tempura, grilled fish, rice, miso soup and pickles, to the ten-course *kaiseki* feasts which must be ordered in advance. The separate sushi menu is recommended.

🏠 197 E1 ✉ Dorland House, 14–20 Lower Regent Street, SW1 ☎ 020 7930 0317; fax: 020 7839 1167 🕐 Mon–Sat noon–2, 6–9:30 🚇 Piccadilly Circus

Nicole's $$

This is a fashionable place in every respect, from the chic setting in the basement of Nicole Farhi's Bond Street store to the ladies-that-lunch who come to toy with the light, ultra-modish food. The restaurant's less figure-conscious clientele will be equally satisfied – an earthier approach can be discerned with such rustic fare as duck confit appearing on the menu. Breakfast is served from 10 to 11.

🏠 196 C2 ✉ 158 New Bond Street, W1 ☎ 020 7499 8408; fax: 020 7409 0381 🕐 Lunch: Mon–Fri noon–3.30, Sat noon–4.30. Dinner: Mon–Fri 6.30– 10.45 🚇 Green Park, Bond Street

Nobu $$$

Nobuyuki Matsuhisa brings the full force of his pan-American experience (which ranges from restaurants in the United States to travels in South America) to bear on the second floor of the seriously chic Metropolitan Hotel. This is the ultimate place to see-and-be-seen, with "A-list" personalities in abundance. The combination of the ultramodern interior and the trendy clientele add up to an irresistible package, especially when New-York-style service and spiced-up Japanese cooking are thrown into the equation. Reservations are essential.

🏠 198 C5 ✉ Metropolitan Hotel, 19 Old Park Lane, W1 ☎ 020 7447 4747; fax: 020 7447 4749 🕐 Lunch: Mon–Fri noon–2:15. Dinner: Mon–Thu 6–10:15, Fri–Sat 6–11 🚇 Hyde Park Corner, Green Park

The Oak Room $$$

The decor is one of Edwardian elegance, enhanced by crystal chandeliers and light-oak paneled walls. Though Marco Pierre White is no longer at the stoves, Robert Reid still heads the brigade. The cooking is modern British at its most accomplished. The strong French classical overtones to the food remain, but the menu structure has been simplified and prices reduced, fortunately without compromising quality. Many of White's signature dishes remain, including the famed pig's trotter "Pierre Koffmann."

✚ 197 E1 ☒ Le Meridien Piccadilly W1 ☎ 020 7437 0202 ☻ Lunch: Mon–Fri noon–2.30. Dinner: Mon–Sat 7–11:15 Ⓔ Piccadilly Circus

Quaglino's $$

Make an entrance down the sweeping staircase, feel the buzz and experience a bit of Hollywood glitz. This is the most glamorous of the Conran mega-restaurants and it's a slick operation. Just go for a drink in the bar or try out a menu that has a strong French bistro feel. If you prefer, traditional English classics such as fish and chips with tartar sauce are on offer. The shellfish bar is a major feature.

✚ 199 D5 ☒ 16 Bury Street, St. James's, SW1 ☎ 020 7930 6767; fax: 020 7839 2866 ☻ Lunch: daily noon–2.30. Dinner: daily 5:30–11 (also Sat 11 pm–1 am, Sun and Mon 11 pm–midnight) Ⓔ Green Park

Rasa W1 $–$$

Das Sreedharan opened this lavish, spacious restaurant after the huge success of his first restaurant in East London. His exquisite vegetarian food from the Kerala region is considered some of the best Indian cooking in town. The menu offers a wide range of poppadums, stuffed pastries, curries, dosas, lentil patties, and some excellent breads.

✚ 196 C2 ☒ 6 Dering Street, W1 ☎ 020 7629 1346 ☻ Lunch: Mon–Sat noon–3. Dinner: Mon–Sat 6–11 Ⓔ Oxford Circus

Sotheby's, The Café $

One of Bond Street's best-kept secrets is tucked away in the lobby of Sotheby's auction house. Join the café's cosmopolitan clientele for stylish breakfasts, light lunches and afternoon tea. Reservations are essential for lunch.

✚ 196 C2 ☒ 34 Bond Street, W1 ☎ 020 7293 5077 ☻ Mon–Fri 9:30–5 Ⓔ Bond Street

The Square $$$

Nigel Platts-Martin's exceptional restaurant combines the allure of chic, spacious premises with a prestigious setting – just a short distance from Berkeley Square. His highly regarded chef and partner, Philip Howard, offers imaginative, yet classically based, modern French cooking. Dishes are prepared with an immense precision and such great attention to detail that it takes in the championing of free-range/organic produce.

✚ 196 C1 ☒ 6 Bruton Street, W1 ☎ 020 7495 7100; fax 020 7495 7150 ☻ Lunch: Mon–Fri noon–2:45. Dinner: Mon–Sat 6:30–10:45, Sun 6:30–9:45 Ⓔ Bond Street

Tamarind $$

This fashionable Indian restaurant serves an imaginative interpretation of Indian regional cooking in its comfortable, discreetly designed basement dining room. Whenever possible, dishes are prepared with specially imported herbs and spices to create some truly memorable flavors.

✚ 198 C5 ☒ 20 Queen Street, W1 ☎ 020 7629 3561; fax: 020 7499 5034 ☻ Lunch: Mon–Fri, Sun noon–3. Dinner: Mon–Sat 6–11:30, Sun 6–10:30 Ⓔ Green Park

Titanic $–$$

This blockbuster restaurant has proved a big hit, especially in the evening when it draws a smart young crowd. There's a large open lobby, a centerpiece bar and a sprawling, noisy dining room.

✚ 197 E1 ☒ 81 Brewer Street, W1 ☎ 020 7437 1912 ☻ Lunch: noon–2:30. Dinner: 5:30–11; bar closes 3 am Ⓔ Green Park

Where to...
Shop

SAVILE ROW AND JERMYN STREET

Savile Row (Tube: Piccadilly Circus) is synonymous with top-quality tailored-to-fit men's clothes. There are several long-established tailors here: Try either **Henry Poole** (15 Savile Row, W1, tel: 020 7734 5985), established in 1806, or **Kilgour, French & Stanbury** (8 Savile Row, W1, tel: 020 7734 6905), dating from 1882.

Jermyn Street (Tube: Piccadilly Circus) has the monopoly on men's shirt makers. Try **Turnbull & Asser** (71–72 Jermyn Street, W1, tel: 020 7930 0502), **Harvie & Hudson** (77 Jermyn Street, W1, tel: 020 7930 3949), and **Hilditch & Key** (73 Jermyn Street, W1, tel: 020 7930 5336).

REGENT STREET

Regent Street (Tube: Piccadilly Circus) is home to stores on a grand scale. **Aquascutum** (100 Regent Street, W1, tel: 020 675 8200) is *the* place to buy the classic English raincoat and tailored, tweedy jackets for both men and women, **Burberrys** (165 Regent Street, W1, tel: 020 7734 4060) is the home of the distinctive English trenchcoat, and **Austin Reed** (103–113 Regent Street, W1, tel: 020 7734 6789) is good for Savile Row-style clothes at rather lower prices.

At the Oxford Circus end of Regent Street is the famed department store **Liberty** (210–220 Regent Street, W1, tel: 020 7734 1234. Tube: Oxford Circus). Even the facade, a mock-Tudor extravaganza, exudes great character. Within, the store is a treasure trove of antiques, oriental carpets, furnishings, dress fabrics and leather goods, as well as cutting-edge fashion, upscale cosmetics and wonderful accessories.

Regent Street is also home to **Hamleys** (188–196 Regent Street, W1, tel: 020 494 2000. Tube: Piccadilly Circus), one of the world's largest toy stores, suitable for kids of all ages. Prices here are higher than elsewhere and on weekends it's packed, but there are magic tricks and demonstrations galore.

PICCADILLY

Occupying a central position on Piccadilly is **Fortnum & Mason** (tel: 020 7734 8040. Tube: Piccadilly Circus). Its internationally renowned food emporium sells everything from own-brand marmalades, teas and condiments to hams, pates, cheeses, bread and fresh fruit. It is also an unusual department store with up-to-date women's designer fashions and a splendid stationery and gift section. The Piccadilly branch of **Waterstones** (203–206 Piccadilly, tel: 020 7851 2400. Tube: Piccadilly Circus), is the place to go if you are looking for a good holiday read.

BOND STREET

Bond Street is a showcase for designers. Fast-paced, upscale fashion is represented in this street by every major international designer, exhibited in their own innovative stores, including **Donna Karan** (19 New Bond Street, W1, tel: 020 7495 3100, Tube: Bond Street). **Gucci** (32–33 Old Bond Street, W1, tel: 020 7629 2716, Tube: Piccadilly Circus) and **Versace** (34–36 Old Bond Street, W1, tel: 020 7499 1862. Tube: Piccadilly Circus).

Also setting out their wares are jewelers such as **Tiffany & Co.** (25 Old Bond Street, W1, tel: 020 7409 2790. Tube: Piccadilly Circus), **Asprey PLC** (167 New Bond Street, W1, tel: 020 493 6767. Tube: Bond Street) and **Cartier** (175 New Bond Street, W1, tel: 020 7493 6962. Tube: Bond Street), two great auction houses, **Sotheby's** (34–35 New Bond Street, W1, tel: 020 293 5000. Tube: Bond Street) and **Phillips** (101 New Bond Street, W1,

Where to...
Be Entertained

You'll find major movie houses and some splendid theaters in the area around Haymarket and Piccadilly Circus. For advice on how to obtain tickets ▶ 160.

MOVIE THEATERS

The **Curzon Mayfair** (38 Curzon Street, W1, tel: 020 7465 8865. Tube: Green Park) shows art-house, foreign and some mainstream movies. **The Institute of Contemporary Arts (ICA)** (Nash House, The Mall, W1, tel: 020 7930 3647. Tube: Charing Cross) has a small movie theater and puts on a program featuring groupings of films that are linked by director, style or theme.

CLUBS

100 Club (100 Oxford Street, W1, tel: 020 7636 0933. Tube: Oxford Circus), where The Rolling Stones, The Kinks, The Sex Pistols and The Clash have all played, follows an eclectic booking policy that also takes in traditional jazz, blues, jive and swing.

COMEDY

If you enjoy hard-hitting stand-up comedy, head for **The Comedy Store** (1a Oxendon Street, W1, recorded information: 020 7344 0234. Tube: Piccadilly Circus). Shows start at 8 pm, but to get the best seats get to the venue when doors open at 6:30 pm.

---

tel: 020 7629 6602. Tube: Bond Street), and major representatives of the art and antiques dealing world, notably the **Fine Art Society** (148 New Bond Street, W1, tel: 020 7629 5116. Tube: Bond Street). Here too is **Fenwick** (63 New Bond Street, W1, tel: 020 7629 9161. Tube: Bond Street), a charming, fashion-oriented department store. The first floor is given over to one of the best accessory collections in town, the basement to a dazzling selection of gifts at less-than-Bond Street prices.

SOUTH MOLTON STREET

On South Molton Street there are smaller, quirkier boutiques, among them **Browns** (23–27 South Molton Street, W1, tel: 020 7491 7833. Tube: Bond Street) – a series of interconnected little stores at the knife-edge of fashion.

Gray's Antique Market (58 Davies Street, W1, tel: 020 7629 7034. Tube: Bond Street) hosts an impressive collection of stalls run by knowledgable people. It's noted for antique jewelry and oriental artifacts, but there is much more.

OXFORD STREET

Oxford Street, big, brash and noisy, with unceasing crowds, is where you'll find most of the big department stores. **John Lewis** (278–306 Oxford Street, W1, tel: 020 7629 7711. Tube: Oxford Circus) sells everything from dress fabrics to computers. **Marks & Spencer**, at both Marble Arch (458 Oxford Street, W1, tel: 020 7935 7954. Tube: Marble Arch) and north of Oxford Circus (173 Oxford Street, W1, tel: 020 7437 7722. Tube: Bond Street) is good for basic wardrobe staples. **Selfridges** (400 Oxford Street, W1, tel: 020 7629 1234. Tube: Bond Street) has Europe's largest perfumery department and a massive cosmetics section, two vast floors of current women's fashions, and a good food hall with various cafes.

The City

Getting Your Bearings

The City of London, the commercial heart of the capital, is one of the busiest financial centers in the world, with banks, corporate headquarters and insurance companies occupying dramatic showcases of modern architecture. Yet alongside the glass-and-steel office buildings, you find beautiful 17th-century churches, cobbled alleyways, historic markets, and even fragments of the original Roman city wall.

The modern City stands on the site of the Roman settlement of *Londinium*, and has long been a center of finance and government. Historically, it had an identity separate to that of the rest of the capital. When Edward the Confessor moved his palace from the City of London to Westminster in 1042, the area retained some of its ancient privileges, and later in the 14th century secured charters granting it the

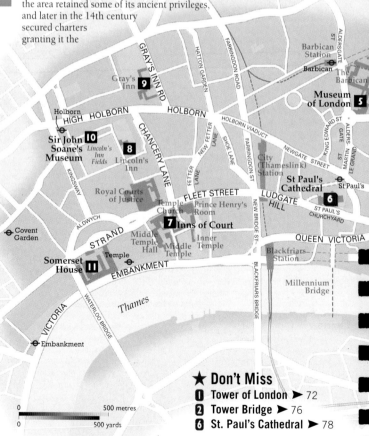

★ **Don't Miss**
1 Tower of London ➤ 72
2 Tower Bridge ➤ 76
6 St. Paul's Cathedral ➤ 78

right to elect its own mayor and council. Even the sovereign could not enter the City without formal permission. Today, the legacy of these privileges still survives. The Corporation of London, the successor to the original council, which is overseen by the Lord Mayor, administers the City through council meetings held in the Guildhall.

Much of the medieval City was destroyed by the Great Fire of 1666, although the Tower of London survived. In the construction boom that followed, architect Sir Christopher Wren was commissioned to build more than 50 churches, the most prominent and well-known of which is St. Paul's Cathedral. Many of the lesser-known Wren churches survived the severe bombing of World War II, and remain tucked away in quiet streets.

The City is also home to the modern Barbican Centre, a performing arts complex, as well as the acclaimed Museum of London, where the story of the capital is brought to life. On the western boundary of the City lie the four historic Inns of Court, the heart of legal London. Next to Lincoln's Inn is Sir John Soane's Museum, a wonderful 19th-century time capsule, while back on the river Somerset House is now home not only to the stunning Courtauld Gallery but also to the glittering treasures of the Gilbert Collection and Hermitage Rooms.

At Your Leisure

Previous page: The distinctive dome of St. Paul's Cathedral

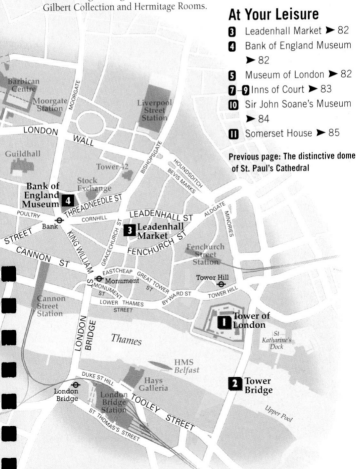

Three of London's most evocative sights – St. Paul's Cathedral, the Tower of London and Tower Bridge – are the day's highlights. Some magnificent views over the city are in store.

The City in a Day

9:00 am

Try to be at the **❶ Tower of London** (➤ 72–75) as it opens (10 am on Sunday) to beat the worst of the crowds, even if this means you may get caught up in the morning rush hour. The rewards are jewels, ravens, Beefeaters (left), and an insight into the long and often bloody history of London from the perspective of its famous fortress. You can buy your entrance ticket in advance from any Underground station.

11:30 am

Walk up on to nearby **❷ Tower Bridge** (below, ➤ 76–77) and visit the Tower Bridge Experience for an excellent history of the structure. Stunning views of the River Thames make the climb to the top worthwhile.

1:00 pm

Take a break for lunch. For top-quality fare head across to the south bank of
the river to **Cantina del Ponte** (➤ 108). Reservations are recommended.

2:15 pm

Walk back across the bridge and catch the No. 15 bus from Tower Hill,
the main road to the north of the Tower, which will deliver you outside
St. Paul's Cathedral.

3:00 pm

Climb up to the galleries at the top of the dome
of ❻ **St. Paul's Cathedral** (below, ➤ 78–81) for
magnificent views of the city. Stop for a coffee
in the café in the crypt. Then soak up the
magnificence of the architecture and
artifacts around you.

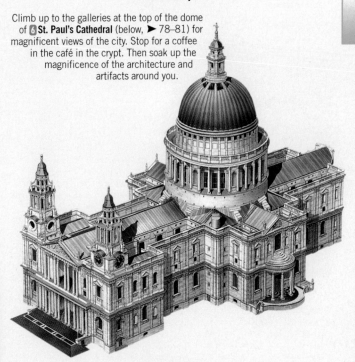

5:00 pm

If possible, stay on in St. Paul's for evensong – the times of services are posted
inside and outside the cathedral.

To move on from St. Paul's catch the No. 15 bus back to Trafalgar Square or
use St. Paul's Underground station, which is just beside the cathedral.

❶ Tower of London

The Tower of London has always fascinated visitors – even 300 years ago it was a popular attraction – and today it is one of the country's top tourist sights. Begun by William the Conqueror shortly after the 1066 conquest, it has survived for over 900 years as a palace, prison, place of execution, arsenal, royal mint and jewel house. Throughout this time it has remained woven into the fabric of London and its history, while maintaining its essential character as a fortress and self-contained world within the defensive walls.

St. Edward's Crown, one of the many priceless treasures making up the Crown Jewels

The Crown Jewels

Begin your exploration of the Tower by visiting Waterloo Barracks, where the Crown Jewels are on display. Lines to see the collection, one of the richest in the world, can be long, but there is archive footage of the Coronation of Queen Elizabeth II to put you in the mood while you wait, providing a prelude to and preview of the exhibition. The most dazzling piece in the collection is the **Imperial State Crown**, used by the monarch at the State Opening of Parliament in October or November, and crusted with 2,868 diamonds, 273 pearls, 17 sapphires, 11 emeralds and 5 rubies. Among the collection's other treasures is the **Sovereign's Sceptre**, which contains the world's largest cut diamond, Cullinan I. Also worth a look is the crown of Queen Elizabeth the Queen Mother. It contains the fabulous Koh-i-Noor diamond, which is only ever used in a woman's crown as it is believed to bring bad luck to men.

For some fascinating background on the Crown Jewels, visit the "Crowns and Diamonds" display in the Martin Tower, accessed via the Salt Tower, whose walls still bear graffiti carved by early prisoners.

✚ 202 C3

✉ Tower Hill, EC3 ☎ 020 7709 0765, www.hrp.org.uk

🕐 Mon–Sat 9–6, Sun 10–6, Apr–Oct; Tue–Sat 9–5, Sun–Mon 10–5, Nov–Mar. Last admission one hour before closing. Closed Jan 1 and Dec 24–26

🍴 Café and restaurant

🚇 Tower Hill 🚌 15, 25 (weekends), 42, 78, 100 💷 Expensive

Tower Green

This benign-looking spot was the place of execution of seven high-ranking prisoners, the most notable of whom were Anne Boleyn and Catherine Howard, Henry VIII's second and fifth wives (both beheaded following charges of adultery). Execution here was an option reserved for the illustrious – less socially elevated prisoners met a much slower, more painful end on nearby Tower Hill. The executioner's axe and block are on display in the White Tower.

The White Tower

The Tower's oldest and most striking feature is the White Tower, begun in about 1078, its basic form having remained unchanged for more than 900 years. Today its highlight is a superlative collection of armor, a display that manages to be awe-inspiring and strangely beautiful at the same time. Henry VIII's personal armor is the main attraction, but smaller pieces,

The Tower of London was begun in 1066, its position affording clear views of any enemy forces that might approach up the Thames

such as the suits crafted for young boys, are equally interesting. Be sure to see the evocative St. John's Chapel on the second floor, one of England's earliest remaining church interiors, and also take a peep into some of the tower's "garderobes" – 11th-century toilets.

The Tower Ravens

Ravens have been associated with the Tower throughout its history. Legend tells how King Charles II wanted to get rid of the birds but was told that if they ever left the White Tower the kingdom would fall and disaster would strike. No chances are taken these days – one wing of each raven is clipped.

The White Tower (1078) is one of the oldest parts of the Tower of London. It took its name after Henry III had its exterior whitewashed in 1241

The Bloody Tower

Not all prisoners in the Tower lived – and died – in terrible conditions. Some passed their time in more humane lodgings. One such prisoner was Sir Walter Ralegh, explorer, philosopher and scientist, who was imprisoned in the Bloody Tower from 1603 to 1616, accused of plotting against James I. The Tower's most notorious incumbents, partly the reason for its name, were the "Princes in the Tower". Following the death of King Edward IV, the princes – the King's sons Edward (the heir to the throne) and his younger brother Richard – were put in the Tower under the "protection" of their uncle, Richard, Duke of

The forbidding walls of the Tower, built to keep attackers out, were later used to confine those perceived to be enemies of the Crown

Beefeaters

The Tower's costumed guards, or Yeoman Warders, are commonly known as Beefeaters, though how they came by the name is not known for certain. About 40 in number, they all have a military background, and perform ceremonial duties around the Tower – they'll also answer your questions and give you directions.

Gloucester. However, the boys mysteriously vanished and, in their absence, their uncle was crowned King Richard III. The skeletons of two boys, presumed to be those of the princes, were found hidden in the White Tower 200 years later. Richard's involvement, or otherwise, in the boys' death has been much debated since but never proved one way or the other.

Traitors' Gate was the Tower of London's entrance from the river

The Medieval Palace

The entrance to the Medieval Palace lies just beside the infamous Traitors' Gate, the river entrance to the Tower through which many prisoners arrived for their execution. The palace is laid out as it would have been in Edward I's reign (1272–1307), and staffed by costumed guides.

From the palace you should stroll along the Wall Walk on the Tower's south side, a route that offers fine views of Tower Bridge (► 76–77). This route also takes you through the Wakefield Tower in whose upper chamber Edward I's throne room has been dramatically reconstructed.

TAKING A BREAK

The cafés of nearby **Leadenhall Market** (► 82) are a great place to stop for a coffee or a light lunch. Alternatively, the Tower has its own restaurant.

TOWER OF LONDON: INSIDE INFO

Top tips Come **early** in the morning to avoid the crowds.
• Buy admission tickets at one of the nearby Tube stations to **avoid the long lines** at the main ticket office.
• On arrival, head straight for the Waterloo Barracks and visit the **Crown Jewels** – this is the Tower's most popular attraction and soon becomes crowded.
• Be **flexible** in your approach to what you visit and when: If one part of the Tower is busy, pass it by and return later.
• If you have time, the Yeoman Warders (Beefeaters) lead free, hour-long **guided tours** throughout the day. Most of the guides are great characters and bring the history of the Tower wonderfully alive.

2 Tower Bridge

Tower Bridge is one of London's most familiar landmarks and the views from its upper walkway are some of the city's best, yet it has occupied its prominent place on the capital's skyline for only a little over a hundred years.

By the late 1800s, crossing the River Thames had become a major problem. London Bridge was then the city's most easterly crossing, but more than a third of the population lived even farther east. Building a new bridge, however, posed a dilemma for architects and planners. Any construction had to allow tall-masted ships to reach the Upper Pool, one of the busiest stretches of river in the world, handling ships and goods from all corners of the British Empire. It also needed to be strong and adaptable enough to allow for the passage of motor and horse-drawn vehicles. Though designs had been submitted to Parliament since the 1850s (over 50 were rejected), it wasn't until 1886 that one was finally approved. The plan for a remarkable lifting roadway (known as a "bascule" bridge after

Top: The floodlit bridge is a prominent feature of the capital's night-time skyline

🞚 202 C2

☎ 020 7940 3985, www.towerbridge.org.uk

🕐 Daily 10–6:30, Apr–Oct; 9:30–6, Nov–Mar. Closed Jan 1 and Dec 24–26. Last entry 75 minutes before closing time

🚇 Tower Hill, London Bridge

🚌 15, 42, 47, 78, 100 ♿ Moderate

VITAL STATISTICS

❏ The bridge took eight years to build.

❏ Its structure is brick and steel, but it is clad in Portland stone
and granite to complement the nearby Tower of London.

❏ Tower Bridge is made up of over 27,000 tons of bricks, enough
to build about 350 detached homes

❏ Each moving bascule weighs 1,200 tons.

❏ The height from the road to the upper walkways is 108 feet.

---

the French word for see-saw), was the brainchild of architect
Horace Jones and engineer John Wolfe Barry.

Access to the bridge's towers and walkways is via the **Tower
Bridge Experience**, an extensive exhibition that includes holograms, animatronic characters, film, artifacts and photographs
to explain the history, construction and operation of the bridge.
You also get to visit the original Victorian engine rooms. The
Experience's highlight, however, is the view from the upper
walkway, where there are also some fascinating archive
photographs, as well as interactive computers offering more
detail on Tower Bridge and the surrounding area.

TAKING A BREAK

If you fancy a treat, head across to the south bank of the river
for lunch at **Cantina del Ponte** (► 108). The food is great, as
are views of the bridge.

TOWER BRIDGE: INSIDE INFO

Top tips Try to see the **bridge lifting**; telephone (020 7940
3984) for times.

• Make a return visit to see the bridge at **night-time** – it looks
fabulous when spot-lit.

• Even if you choose not to experience "The Experience," don't
miss the magnificent view from either of the bridge's piers.

6 St. Paul's Cathedral

The towering dome of St. Paul's Cathedral has stood sentinel over London for almost 300 years, a lasting testament to the revolutionary genius of its architect, Sir Christopher Wren. Innovative and controversial, the cathedral rose from the ashes of the Great Fire of London in the 17th century, making it a positive youngster when compared with the medieval cathedrals of most European countries. Centuries later it became a symbol of London's unbeatable spirit, standing proud throughout the wartime Blitz of 1940–41, while more recently it has been the scene of national events such as the wedding of Prince Charles to Diana, Princess of Wales (then Lady Diana Spencer) in 1981.

The present cathedral, completed in 1710, is the fourth on this site

The entrance to the cathedral is in the **West Front** between the towers. Be prepared for noise and crowds, and remember the cathedral is enormous.

On first entering the cathedral, take a few moments to just stand and soak up something

🕂 201 E4
☎ 020 7236 4128, www.stpauls.co.uk
✉ Ludgate Hill, EC4
🕐 Mon–Sat 8:30–4:30 (last admission 4 pm) 🍴 Café in the crypt.
🚇 St. Paul's 🚌 4, 11, 15, 17, 23, 26, 76, 100, 172, 521
💷 Moderate; free for Sun service

VITAL STATISTICS

❏ The cathedral's largest bell, Great Paul, which weighs 17 tons, is rung at 1 pm every day for 5 minutes.

❏ The distance from ground level to the very top of the cross on the cathedral's roof measures just short of 368 feet.

❏ The clock, Big Tom, on the right-hand tower on the cathedral's West Front, is almost the same size as the clock at Big Ben. The clock face is 16 feet in diameter and the minute hand 10 feet long.

Monochrome frescoes depicting the life of St. Paul decorate the interior of the dome

of the building's grandeur. Soaring arches lead the eye toward the huge open space below the main dome, and on to a series of smaller, brilliantly decorated domes that rise above the choir and distant high altar.

Then move to the center of the nave, marked by an intricate black-and-white compass pattern and a memorial to Wren which includes the line "Reader, if you seek his monument, look around you." Looking up into the **dome** from here you

can admire the Whispering Gallery, the monochrome frescoes by 18th-century architectural painter Sir James Thornhill (1716–19) of the life of St. Paul, and the windows in the upper lantern. Wren was 75 years old by the time the upper lantern was underway but still insisted on being hauled up to the galleries in a basket several times a week to check on progress. What he wouldn't have seen are the ceiling's shimmering mosaics, completed in the 1890s, and made from an estimated 30 million or more pieces of glass. They depict biblical scenes and figures such as Evangelists, prophets, the Creation, the Garden of Eden and the Crucifixion.

Then take in the area around the **altar**, a part of the cathedral filled with exquisite works of art. Master woodcarver Grinling Gibbons, noted for his high relief carvings, designed the limewood choir stalls – the cherubs are especially fine – and Jean Tijou, a Huguenot refugee, created the intricate ironwork gates (both were completed in 1720). The canopy is based on a similar bronze canopy in St. Peter's, Rome, designed by the 16th-century baroque architect Bernini. In St. Paul's, however, the canopy is made of English oak and dates from as recently as 1958.

The Galleries
The dome has three galleries, all of them open to the public and all unmissable if you've the time, energy and a head for heights. The views of the cathedral's interior and of London are breathtaking – but there are over 500 steps to climb to the top before you can enjoy them. The best interior views come from the **Whispering Gallery** (259 steps), where the building's patterned floor and sheer scale can be enjoyed to the full. The gallery's name describes the strange acoustic effect that allows something said on one side of the gallery to be heard on the other. For panoramas of London you'll need to climb to the top two galleries, the **Stone Gallery** (378 steps from the bottom) and the **Golden Gallery** (a further 172 steps).

At the other extreme, downstairs, is the crypt, a peaceful and atmospheric space supported by massive piers and redoubtable vaulting. This is the largest such crypt in Europe, and contains around 200 graves and memorials, the grandest of which belong to national heroes such as Admiral Lord Nelson and the Duke of Wellington, who defeated Napoleon at the battle of Waterloo in 1815.

The Whispering Gallery, where whispers on one side of the gallery can be heard on the other

TAKING A BREAK
St. Paul's own Refectory restaurant (tel: 020 7246 8358, open 11–5:30), in the crypt, is an ideal place to stop for a light lunch or afternoon tea.

ST PAUL'S CATHEDRAL: INSIDE INFO

Top tips Guided tours (90 min.–120 min.; additional charge) run at 11, 11:30, 1:30 and 2. Cassette tours are also available.

Hidden gem The choir, one of the finest in the world, sings on Sunday at 11 am and 5:15 pm. **Evensong** on weekdays is usually at 5 pm, but check the lists posted at the cathedral for more information or call 020 7236 4128 for details.

At Your Leisure

3 Leadenhall Market

This iron-and-glass Victorian food hall, built on the site of an ancient medieval market, now caters to the needs of City workers, with plenty of eating places, tailors, shoe stores, bookstores, pharmacies and grocers. The huge glass roof and finely renovated and painted iron work, plus the bustle of the crowds, make this one of the best places in the City to browse, grab a snack or linger over lunch.

🚇 202 B4 ✉ Whittington Avenue, EC3 🕐 Mon–Fri 7–4 🚇 Monument 🚌 25, 40

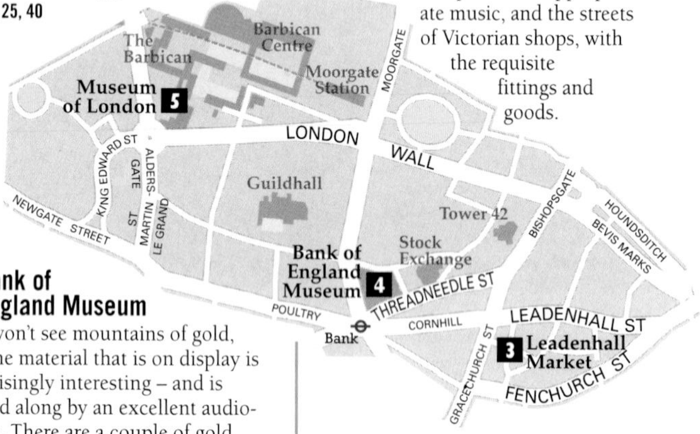

5 Museum of London

This fascinating museum details the story of London from prehistoric times to the present day, its magnificent array of information and exhibits laid out chronologically to present a cogent and colorful account of the city's evolution.

The Roman Gallery is particularly well illustrated, and includes excellent reconstructions of Roman-era rooms. Look also for the paneled Stuart interior of a prosperous merchant's home, complete with appropriate music, and the streets of Victorian shops, with the requisite fittings and goods.

[map showing the City area: The Barbican, Barbican Centre, Museum of London 5, Moorgate Station, MOORGATE, LONDON WALL, Guildhall, KING EDWARD ST, ALDERS-GATE ST, MARTIN'S LE GRAND, NEWGATE STREET, Tower 42, Stock Exchange, Bank of England Museum 4, POULTRY, Bank, CORNHILL, THREADNEEDLE ST, BISHOPSGATE, HOUNDSDITCH, BEVIS MARKS, LEADENHALL ST, Leadenhall Market 3, GRACECHURCH ST, FENCHURCH ST]

4 Bank of England Museum

You won't see mountains of gold, but the material that is on display is surprisingly interesting – and is helped along by an excellent audioguide. There are a couple of gold ingots on show which always draw a big crowd, but more fascinating are the displays explaining how bank notes are printed and the complex security devices employed to beat counterfeiters. If you fancy yourself as a financial whizz-kid, there are interactive computer programs that allow you to simulate trading on the foreign exchange markets – after a few minutes trying to get to grips with the processes you can see how real City superstars begin to justify their huge salaries.

🚇 202 A4 ✉ Bartholomew Lane, EC2 ☎ 020 7601 5545 🕐 Mon–Fri 10–5 🚇 Bank 🚌 8, 21, 23, 25, 43, 76, 133, 242 🎫 Free

On a smaller scale, the working model of the Great Fire of London, accompanied by the words of Samuel Pepys, is an excellent illustration of the drama of this cataclysmic event (▶ 6–7). Perhaps the most gorgeous exhibit, however, is the Lord Mayor's Coach, commissioned in 1757. A confection of color and ornament, it is covered in magnificent carvings and sculptures and has panels by the Florentine artist Cipriani decorating its sides. The coach is still used during the annual Lord Mayor's Parade in November and the coronation of a new sovereign.

🚇 201 F5 ✉ London Wall ☎ 020 7600 3699; www.museumoflondon.org.uk

The elaborately carved and gilded Lord Mayor's Coach, one of the exhibits at the Museum of London

🕐 Mon–Sat 10–5:50, Sun noon–5:50; last admission 5:30. Closed Jan 1 and Dec 24–26 🍴 Café 🚇 St. Paul's, Barbican 🚌 4, 56, 100 🎫 Free

🔟–🔟 Inns of Court

Entered through narrow, easy-to-miss gateways, the four Inns of Court are a world away from the busy city outside. Their ancient buildings, well-kept gardens and hushed atmosphere create an aura of quiet industry. Home to London's legal profession, the Inns began life in the 14th century as hostels where lawyers stayed. Until the 19th century, the only way to obtain legal qualifications was to serve an apprenticeship at the Inns, and even today advocates must be members of an Inn.

While most of the buildings are private, some are open to the public; even if you don't see inside any of the venerable institutions it is enough simply to wander the small lanes and cobbled alleyways, stumbling upon unexpected courtyards and gardens and breathing the rarefied legal air.

The way to see the Inns is to start at the Temple and then walk to Lincoln's Inn and Gray's Inn.

For Kids
- Tower of London (➤ 72–75)
- St. Paul's Cathedral galleries (➤ 78–81)
- Museum of London (➤ 82)

Inner and Middle Temple

Consecrated in 1185, Temple Church originally had links with the Knights Templar, a confraternity of soldier monks established to protect pilgrims traveling to the Holy Land. This may account for the building's unusual circular plan, which mirrors that of the Church of the Holy Sepulchre in Jerusalem. The floor of the church has ancient effigies of the Knights' patrons, though few date from after the 13th century as the Knights fell out of favor and were abolished in 1312. The church is a tranquil oasis in a busy part of the city.

The imposing **Middle Temple Hall,** where it is said Queen Elizabeth I attended the first performance of Shakespeare's *Twelfth Night,* retains its 16th-century oak-paneled interior.

➕ 200 C4 ✉ Access from Fleet Street, just opposite end of Chancery Lane, EC4 🕐 Temple Church: Wed–Sun 11–4; Middle Temple Hall: usually Mon–Fri 10:30–noon, 2:30–4. Phone in advance to confirm. ☎ 020 7427 4800

Prince Henry's Room

This remarkable little building – above the Fleet Street entrance to the Temple – was built in 1610 as part of a Fleet Street tavern. The room, decorated to commemorate the investiture of Henry, eldest son of James I, as Prince of Wales, retains the ceiling inscribed with the Prince of Wales' feathers and part of its original oak paneling. It houses memorabilia associated with the diarist Samuel Pepys (1633–1703), who lived locally but who was not directly associated with the building.

➕ 200 C4 ✉ 17 Fleet Street, EC4 🕐 Mon–Sat 11–2

Lincoln's Inn

Lincoln's Inn is large, well maintained and spacious, and its red-brick buildings are constructed on a grand scale, particularly the four-storied mansions, New Hall and library of New Square (begun in 1680). Many illustrious British politicians studied here, among them Pitt the Younger, Walpole, Disraeli, Gladstone and Asquith. Other former students include William Penn, founder of Pennsylvania, and 17th-century poet John Donne. Make a special point of seeing the Inn's chapel (Mon–Fri noon–2:30), built above a beautiful undercroft with massive pillars and dramatic vaulting.

➕ 200 C4 ✉ Entrances off Chancery Lane and Lincoln's Inn Fields, WC2 🕐 Mon–Fri 7–7

Gray's Inn

Entrances off High Holborn, Gray's Inn Road, Theobald's Road, WC1. This Inn dates from the 14th century but was much restored after damage during World War II. Famous names to have passed through its portals include the writer Charles Dickens, who was a clerk here between 1827 and 1828. Its highlights are the extensive gardens or "Walks" as they are commonly known (Mon–Fri noon–2:30), once the setting for some infamous duels and where diarist Samuel Pepys used to admire the ladies promenading. The chapel is also open to the public (Mon–Fri 10–6) but lacks the charm of its Lincoln's Inn equivalent (see above).

➕ 200 C5

🔟 Sir John Soane's Museum

When 19th-century gentleman, architect and art collector Sir John Soane died in 1837, he left his home and its contents to the nation. The only condition of his bequest was that nothing was altered. The resulting museum, a charming artistic and social showcase, has remained unchanged for 150 years.

Soane's passion was for collecting; a passion that seems to have been more or less unchecked or unguided – he simply bought whatever caught his eye. As a result, the house is packed with a miscellany of beautiful, but eclectic objects, with ceramics, books, paintings, statues, even a skeleton, jostling for space. One of the collection's highlights is the ancient Egyptian sarcophagus of Pharaoh Seti I, carved from a single block of limestone and engraved with scenes from the afterlife to guide the soul of the deceased.

For many years this eccentric jewel was known only to the well-informed few. Now that the secret is out, you can expect more people; come early or late on weekdays to avoid the worst crowds.

➕ 200 B5 ✉ 13 Lincoln's Inn Fields, WC2 ☎ 020 7405 2107; www.soane.org 🕐 Tue–Sat 10–5 (also first Tue of month 6–9 pm with some rooms candlelit). Groups of six or more must book in advance 🚇 Holborn 🚌 1, 8, 25, 68, 91, 168, 171, 188, 242 🎟 Free

A beautiful miscellany: Sir John Soane's eclectic collection

🔟 Somerset House

Once the repository of British citizens' birth, marriage and death records, this majestic riverside building is now home to three superb art collections.

The most famous is the long-established **Courtauld Gallery**, whose reputation rests largely on its collection of Impressionist and Post-Impressionist paintings, which includes works by Cézanne, Seurat, Gauguin, Renoir, Monet, Manet (*Bar at the Folies-Bergère*), Toulouse-Lautrec and Van Gogh (*Self-Portrait with a Bandaged Ear*). Rooms on the lower floors contain earlier paintings, many of them religious works. The 15th-century *Triptych* by the Master of Flemalle (Room 1) and *Adam and Eve* by Lucas Cranach the Elder (1526) are among the highlights.

The **Gilbert Collection**, an extraordinarily beautiful exhibition of decorative arts, focuses in particular on snuff boxes and micro-mosaics. The subject matter may not seem promising, but many of the exhibits are breathtaking in the degree of technical virtuosity. Huge gold and silver items, jeweled chalices and a pair of quite amazing golden church gates are other highlights.

The **Hermitage Rooms** display rotating exhibitions of world-class paintings and other objects on loan from the famous St. Petersburg museum.

➕ 200 B3 ✉ Strand WC2 🍴 Café, Admiralty restaurant 🚇 Temple (closed Sun), Embankment or Covent Garden 🚌 1, 4, 6, 9, 11, 13, 15, 23, 26, 76, 77A, 91, 168, 171, 171A, 176, 188

Courtauld Gallery
☎ 020 7848 2922; www.courtauld.ac.uk 🕐 Mon–Sat 10–6, Sun and public holidays noon–6. Closed Jan 1, Dec 24–26 🖐 Moderate, free to under 18s, joint ticket available with Gilbert Collection

Gilbert Collection
☎ 020 7240 9400; www.gilbert-collection.org.uk 🕐 Mon–Sat 10–6, Sun and public holidays noon–6. Closed Jan 1, Dec 24–26 🖐 Moderate, free to under 18s, free 10–2 Mon, joint ticket available with Courtauld Gallery

Hermitage Rooms
☎ 020 7845 4630; www.hermitagerooms.com 🕐 Mon–Sat 10–6, Sun and public holidays noon–6. Closed Jan 1, Dec 24–26 🖐 Moderate. Tickets sold for timed slots on the hour and half-hour

Where to...
Eat and Drink

Prices
Expect to pay per person for a meal excluding drinks and service
$** under £25 **$$** £25–£50 **$$$ over £50

Alba $–$$

This smart, modern Italian restaurant, just a short walk from the Barbican Centre, provides excellent value for money and is deservedly popular. It is filled with business people at lunchtime and theater-goers in the evening.

The menu is sensibly short, encouraging some serious cooking. Fish or meat dishes, such as Trentino lamb stew, and classics like chicken cacciatore are prepared with first-rate ingredients. The annotated wine list gives an impressive selection of wines from the best Italian vineyards.

➕ Off map 201 F5 ✉ 107 Whitecross Street, EC1 ☎ 020 7588 1798; fax: 020 7638 5793 🕐 Mon–Fri noon–2:30, 6–11; closed 10 days Christmas, public holidays
Ⓜ Barbican

1 Blossom Street $$

A sheltered garden forms the entrance to this smart, spacious basement restaurant in a surprisingly quiet residential area close to Liverpool Street. The open-to-view kitchen relies on seasonal produce, which places the emphasis firmly on flavor. The result is a short set menu with strong Mediterranean leanings. The wine list is wide-ranging and a good value. Service is relaxed but professional.

➕ Off map 202 C5 ✉ 1 Blossom Street E1 ☎ 020 7247 6530 🕐 Mon–Fri noon–3, 6–9 (bar open all day); closed Sat–Sun Ⓜ Liverpool Street

City Rhodes $$$

At City Rhodes, television celebrity chef Gary Rhodes has created an upscale setting in which to sample his reworking of classic English dishes. The well-spaced, sparsely decorated room comes with a pricey menu, but the cooking is first class. Stunning presentation stirs up the appetite and old-fashioned ingredients are frequently given a new spin. Dessert should not be missed; bread-and-butter pudding is a signature dish. The service is well-paced, enthusiastic and efficient. Highly recommended.

➕ 201 D1 ✉ 1 New Street Square, EC4 ☎ 020 7583 1313; fax: 020 7353 1662 🕐 Mon–Fri noon–2:30, 6–8:45 Ⓜ Blackfriars

Club Gascon $$–$$$

Pascal Aussignac, from Toulouse in Southwest France, has rapidly established a name for himself in this gastronomically evolving part of London. He offers top-class Gascon cooking with the emphasis on *foie gras* and duck, ingredients which are supplied direct by French farmers and producers in Gascony. Although traditionally prepared dishes are Aussignac's specialties, he is not afraid to experiment. Tables may be cramped but the atmosphere at Club Gascon is vibrant. Highly recommended. Booking is essential.

➕ 201 E5 ✉ 57 West Smithfield, EC1 ☎ 020 7796 0600 🕐 Lunch: Mon–Fri noon–1:45. Dinner: Mon–Thu 7–9:45, Fri 7–10:15, Sat 7:30–10:30 Ⓜ Farringdon

The Eagle $–$$

The Eagle was one of the pioneers of converted pubs specializing in very good food and still leads the field. Choose from a short, but mouth-watering selection of mainly Spanish- and Portuguese-influenced dishes; all are great value for money. Reservations are not taken and as this establishment is lively and often crowded, you need to arrive early to secure a table and have the best choice from the blackboard. You order and pay for your food and drink at the bar.

➕ Off map 201 D5 ⊠ 159 Farringdon Road, EC1 ☎ 020 7837 1353 ◉ Lunch: Mon–Fri noon–2:30 (also Sat 2:30–3:30, Sun 2–4). Dinner: Mon–Fri 6:30–10:30, Sat 6–10:30 Ⓔ Farringdon

Maison Novelli $$–$$$

Imaginative cooking pioneered by Jean-Christophe Novelli matches the panache of the smart, bright dining room, which is filled with fresh flowers, big mirrors and bold blue-purple colors. Novelli classics such as stuffed braised pig's trotter and hot-and-cold chocolate pudding are never off the menu, but there are plenty of daring combinations

using Asian, oriental and European influences. Next door, Novelli EC1 offers a less expensive alternative.

➕ Off map 201 D5 ⊠ 29 Clerkenwell Green, EC1 ☎ 020 7251 6606; fax: 020 7490 1083 ◉ Lunch: Mon–Fri noon–3. Dinner: Mon–Sat 6–11 Ⓔ Farringdon

Moro $$

The opening of this restaurant caused a great frisson of excitement among the capital's food critics. The minimalist decor with a long zinc bar down one wall, an open-plan kitchen along another, and plain, close-packed wooden tables creates an informal setting. The food is magical, largely Spanish and North African in origin, with good raw materials simply cooked in a wood-burning oven or charbroiled. Reservations need to be made well in advance.

➕ Off map 201 D5 ⊠ 34–36 Exmouth Market, EC1 ☎ 020 7833 8336; fax: 020 7833 9338 ◉ Mon–Fri 12:30–2:30, 7–10:30 Ⓔ Farringdon

Quality Chop House $$

Much of the original character of this informal former Victorian chop house has been preserved, including high-backed mahogany booths. The food is a fashionable mix of updated traditional English dishes and French brasserie classics, with eggs, bacon and fries, fish soup with *rouille*, confit of duck, and Toulouse sausage with mashed potato and onion gravy never off the menu. No credit cards are taken.

➕ Off map 201 D5 ⊠ 94 Farringdon Road, EC1 ☎ 020 7837 5093 ◉ Lunch: Mon–Fri noon–3, Sun noon–4. Dinner: Mon–Sat 6:30–11, Sun 7–11 Ⓔ Farringdon, King's Cross

St. John $$

Back-to-basics eating is the principle behind this Clerkenwell hotspot close to Smithfield. The decor of the former smokehouse is starkly white and minimalist, and an open-plan kitchen adds to the general informality. Traditional old English recipes are reworked – offal is

greatly favored – and sit happily alongside modern Mediterranean dishes on the short menu. The kitchen adopts a simple approach, using prime fresh produce.

➕ 201 E5 ⊠ 26 St. John Street, EC1 ☎ 020 7251 0848, 020 7251 4998; fax: 020 7251 4090 ◉ Lunch: Mon–Fri noon–3. Dinner: Mon–Sat 6–11 Ⓔ Farringdon

BARS

Cicada $

At this minimalist bar/restaurant, drinkers frequently outnumber those eating in the evening. The young, stylish clientele create an atmosphere that is lively, noisy and fun. The food, should you wish to eat here, is oriental in style, backed up by some excellent, inexpensive wines from a list that includes chilled *sake* by the flask.

➕ Off map ⊠ 132–136 St. John Street, EC1 ☎ 020 7608 1550 ◉ Mon–Fri noon–3, 6–11 Ⓔ Farringdon

Where to...
Shop

The City of London is not a significant shopping area, particularly when compared with other parts of the capital.

Stores in the City are geared to the needs of office workers, and sandwich bars, wine bars and pubs dominate, with a few tourist gift shops near the City sights. However, the few **markets** that remain in this part of London have strong historic and social roots and make an enjoyable outing.

Columbia Road Flower Market
(Columbia Road, E2, open Sun 8–2. Tube: Old Street) is where many Londoners come to stock up with plants for their terraces and window boxes. Even if you don't want to

buy a massive yucca or tray of begonias, it's worth a visit.

Petticoat Lane market
(Middlesex Street and beyond, E1, open Sun 9–2. Tube: Aldgate) is an East London institution. It's *the* place to buy inexpensive clothes and shoes. However, coachloads of tourists add to the crush and make browsing difficult. The end of the market by Aldgate East Underground station is devoted to leather jackets; it is possible to get a bargain if you are prepared to haggle. Take cash, not credit cards, to get the best deal.

The giant Victorian covered marketplace at **Spitalfields Market** (Commercial Street between Lamb Street and Brushfield Street, E1, open Mon–Fri 11–3, Sun 9:30–5. Tube: Liverpool Street) is filled with interesting craft stalls and an array of fast-food outlets selling a range of foods from crepes to sushi and tandoori. The market has a very good organic food section every Friday and Sunday.

Where to...
Be Entertained

Much of the City remains quiet in the evenings. The Barbican Centre and Broadgate Centre are the area's focal points.

When the **Barbican Centre** (Silk Street, EC2. Box Office tel: 020 7638 8891; general information tel: 020 7638 4141) first opened, journalists wrote critical reviews about how difficult it was for concert-goers to find their way around this behemoth in a featureless part of the City. Music and theater-lovers crowd in, however, lured by the center's proximity to Clerkenwell, London's latest culinary hotspot, as well as by the cultural program.

The Barbican is the home of the London Symphony Orchestra, who offer 85 concerts a year with

performances by some of the worlds top musicians, as well as two theaters and two movie screens, where you can see the latest releases.

It's well worth dropping by the Barbican's lobby, especially on weekends when a variety of free entertainment is on offer. There are also various cafes on the different levels. The Barbican is best reached by Underground. Barbican and Moorgate stations are the closest, and have the bonus of clearly marked directions to the complex.

At the **Broadgate Centre** (Broadgate Circus, Eldon Street, EC2. Tube: Moorgate) tiers of stores and restaurants line an impressive amphitheater, where you can go ice-skating in winter and enjoy open-air entertainment in summer.

Westminster and the South Bank

Getting Your Bearings

Stand on one of the bridges or embankments and as you gaze at the slowly flowing River Thames you can't help but notice the contrast between the water's stately progress and the noise and drama of the surrounding city.

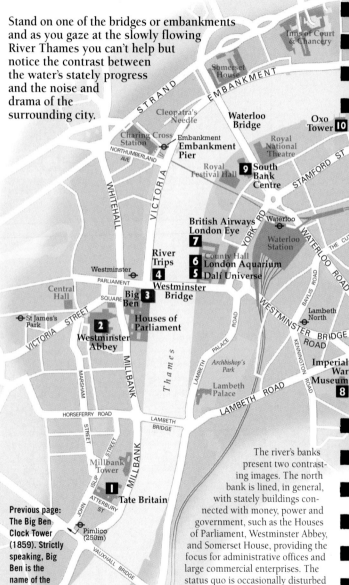

Inns of Court & Chancery

Somerset House

STRAND

EMBANKMENT

Cleopatra's Needle

Waterloo Bridge

Oxo Tower **10**

Charing Cross Station

Embankment Pier

Embankment

Royal National Theatre

NORTHUMBERLAND AVE

Royal Festival Hall

9 South Bank Centre

STAMFORD ST

WHITEHALL

VICTORIA

British Airways London Eye **7**

YORK RD

Waterloo

Waterloo Station

THE CUT

WATERLOO ROAD

River Trips **4**

County Hall

6 London Aquarium

5 Dalí Universe

BAYLIS ROAD

Westminster

PARLIAMENT

Westminster Bridge

Central Hall

SQUARE

Big Ben **3**

Houses of Parliament

Lambeth North

WESTMINSTER BRIDGE ROAD

St James's Park

VICTORIA STREET

2

Westminster Abbey

PALACE ROAD

LAMBETH

Archbishop's Park

KENNINGTON ROAD

Imperial War Museum

8

MARSHAM

MILLBANK

Thames

Lambeth Palace

LAMBETH ROAD

HORSEFERRY ROAD

LAMBETH BRIDGE

STREET

Millbank Tower

MILLBANK

ISLIP

Tate Britain

ATTERBURY ST

1

Pimlico (250m)

JOHN

STREET

VAUXHALL BRIDGE

Previous page: The Big Ben Clock Tower (1859). Strictly speaking, Big Ben is the name of the 13-ton bell

The river's banks present two contrasting images. The north bank is lined, in general, with stately buildings connected with money, power and government, such as the Houses of Parliament, Westminster Abbey, and Somerset House, providing the focus for administrative offices and large commercial enterprises. The status quo is occasionally disturbed by new buildings – Charing Cross train station is a notable example – but generally the river's north side is stable and established, retaining the political, historical and religious significance it has enjoyed for centuries.

The South Bank has a very different flavor. In Shakespeare's time it was the place to which actors were banished and where early theater flourished. The reborn Globe is turning the clock back 400 years. By the early 20th century the area was a mixture of waste-

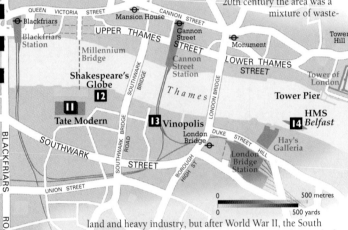

land and heavy industry, but after World War II, the South Bank Centre, and the Royal Festival Hall in particular, marked the start of a makeover. Continuing the shift, as London entered the new millennium, the old Bankside Power Station was transformed from industrial behemoth to cultural superstar in the shape of the Tate Modern gallery. Yet even Tate Modern has been eclipsed in popularity and profile by the surprise success of of the British Airways London Eye. This elegant, slow-motion big wheel has rapidly become one of London's hottest tickets and is the perfect vantage point for planning your itinerary.

Art, religion, the world's most famous clock and a famously scenic river walk form the heart of this day's sightseeing. Note that Westminster Abbey closes early on Saturday and is open on Sunday only for services.

Westminster and the South Bank in a Day

9:30 am

Allow two hours to enjoy the grandeur of **2 Westminster Abbey** (right, ➤ 94–97), looking out for the numerous memorials to royal and literary figures among breathtaking architecture, particularly the Royal Chapels.

11:30 am

Admire the **3 Houses of Parliament** and **3 Big Ben** (➤ 98–99), cross **3 Westminster Bridge** and make a left, toward the landmark **7 British Airways London Eye** (➤ 104). Here you are spoiled for choice, with the Eye, the **6 London Aquarium** (➤ 104) and the **5 Dalí Universe** (➤ 103) all vying for your time and money. Note: trips on the London Eye should be booked in advance.

1:30 pm

Stroll along the river to the **Royal Festival Hall**,
where you can enjoy an informal lunch in the
fourth-floor People's Palace (➤ 109), while
admiring the views of the Thames.

2:00 pm

Browse in the designer workshops of the
10 **Oxo Tower** (➤ 105) and if you have not
already had an eyeful of the Thames take
the elevator to the top to the Oxo Tower's
free viewing platform.

3:00 pm

Make your way to 11 **Tate Modern** (➤ 100–101), London's latest modern art
gallery, set in the former Bankside Power Station (below). Choose a couple of

galleries rather than trying to
see the whole collection and,
if you can, join one of the
excellent free guided tours.
If you have any energy left,
12 **Shakespeare's Globe**
(➤ 106), a reconstruction of
the original Globe Theatre, is
just a short walk away. If
you've timed it right, you
could finish off your day by
seeing a play here.

② Westminster Abbey

Britain's greatest religious building is a church, a national shrine, the setting for coronations and a burial place for some of the most celebrated figures from almost a thousand years of British history. Most of the country's sovereigns, from William the Conqueror to Queen Elizabeth II, have been crowned (and buried) at Westminster, while in 1997 it was the setting for the funeral of Diana, Princess of Wales. The building has ancient roots, but construction of the present structure, a masterpiece of medieval architecture, began in the 13th century. Since then the building has grown and evolved, a process that continues to the present day as ever more modern memorials are erected.

Westminster Abbey is one of London's top tourist destinations, drawing huge crowds. It's impossible to appreciate all the abbey's abundance of riches in one visit, so concentrate on the selected highlights below.

Visitors follow a set route around the abbey. From the entrance through the North Door you head first along the ambulatory, the passageway leading to the far end of the abbey. At the top of the steps, the chapel on the left contains the **tomb of Elizabeth I** (1533–1603) and her older half-sister, Mary Tudor (1516–58), daughters of the much-married Henry VIII. Although they lie close in death, there was little love lost beween them in life – Mary was a Catholic, Elizabeth a Protestant at a time when religious beliefs

---

Left: The nave and vaulting of Westminster Abbey

Above: The West Towers

✚ 199 F4 ✉ Broad Sanctuary, SW1 ☎ 020 7222 5152; www.westminster-abbey.org
🕐 Mon–Fri 9:30–4:45, Sat 9–2:45. Last admission 1 hour before closing. Sun open for worship only. College Garden: Tue–Thu 10–6, Apr–Sep; 10–4, Oct–Mar
🍴 Coffee counter in cloisters and Broad Sanctuary
🚇 Westminster, St. James's Park 🚌 3, 11, 12, 24, 53, 77A, 88, 159, 211
🎟 Moderate

divided the country and religious persecution was rife.

Next comes the sublime **Henry VII Chapel** built in 1512, possibly to ease Henry's troubled conscience: His route to the throne was a violent one. The abbey's most gorgeous chapel, it was described by one commentator as *orbis miraculum*, or a wonder of the world. The brilliantly detailed and gilded fan vaulting of the roof is particularly splendid, as are the vivid banners of the Knights of the Order of the Bath (an order of chivalry bestowed by the monarch) above the oak choir stalls. Behind the altar are the magnificent tombs and gilded effigies of Henry VII and his wife, Elizabeth, created to a personal design by Henry himself.

Breathtakingly delicate fan vaulting in the Henry VII Chapel

As you leave this area, a side chapel holds the tomb of Mary, Queen of Scots (1542–87). Mary, a rival to Elizabeth I's throne, was imprisoned for 19 years before finally being executed in 1587. Mary's son, James VI of Scotland, became James I of England when the unmarried, childless Elizabeth died. He had his mother's body exhumed and brought to the abbey 25 years after her death and erected the monuments to both Elizabeth I and Mary – but his mother's is much the grander.

WILLIAM SHAKESPEARE 1564 ~ 1616
BURIED AT STRATFORD-ON-AVON

NOËL COWARD
Playwright · Actor · Composer
16 December 1899
26 March 1973
Buried in Jamaica
'A TALENT TO AMUSE'

Poets' Corner Notables

Alfred, Lord Tennyson
Dylan Thomas
Henry James
T. S. Eliot
George Eliot
William Wordsworth
Jane Austen
The Brontë sisters

As you go back down the stairs don't miss the unassuming chair facing you. This is the **Coronation Chair**, dating from 1296, and has been used at the coronation of most British monarchs. For several centuries anyone could sit on it: Many who did left their mark in the form of graffiti.

Next comes **Poets' Corner**, packed with the graves and memorials of literary superstars. You'll spot Geoffrey Chaucer, author of *The Canterbury Tales*; Shakespeare, commemorated by a memorial (he is buried

The Battle of Britain window contains the badges of the 65 fighter squadrons who took part in that World War II battle

in Stratford-upon-Avon); and Charles Dickens, who was buried here against his wishes on the orders of Queen Victoria. Thomas Hardy's ashes are here, but his heart was buried in Dorset, the setting for many of his novels.

From Poets' Corner, walk toward the center of the abbey and the highly decorated altar and choir stalls. One of the loveliest views in the abbey opens up from the steps leading to the altar, looking along the length of the nave to the window above the West Door. For a restful interlude head into the 13th-century **cloisters**, a covered passageway around a small garden once used for reflection by the abbey's monks. Contemplation is also the effect created by the simple black slab memorial at the western end of the abbey – the **Tomb of the Unknown Soldier**, an eloquent testimony to the dead of war.

WESTMINSTER ABBEY: INSIDE INFO

Top tips Attend a **choral service** to see the abbey at its best. Evensong is at 5 pm on weekdays. Times of other services are displayed, otherwise call for details.
• **Guided tours** led by abbey vergers leave several times daily (90 min., additional charge). Book at the information desk. There is also an **audio guide**, available in several languages, which provides good additional background (charge).

In more detail Off the cloisters, explore the beautiful 13th-century **Chapter House**, the **Pyx Chamber**, also a survivor of the original fabric, and the **Abbey Museum** with its fascinating wax effigies of royalty (additional charges).

Hidden gems The **College Garden**, open Tuesdays to Thursdays, is a haven of tranquillity. Access is from the cloisters, via the delightful Little Cloister.
• Look for the new **statues above the West Door**. These celebrate modern Christian martyrs from around the world.

3 The Thames

This short, but panoramic walk takes in Westminster and Waterloo bridges and some of the best sights of the river's south and north banks. It offers an opportunity to appreciate a selection of London's finest views and a chance to enjoy a different outlook on examples of the capital's historical and more modern architecture.

Start on the north bank in front of the **Houses of Parliament** (a complex officially known as the Palace of Westminster), which is the country's seat of government. Much of the structure was rebuilt in the 19th century following a fire, but Westminster Hall, part of the original palace, dates from 1097. The Victoria Tower (335 feet tall) stands at one end and the tower holding Big Ben (322 feet tall) at the other. Strictly speaking **Big Ben** is the name of the tower's 13-ton bell, not the tower itself. How the name was coined is uncertain – the bell may have been named after the heavyweight boxing champion, Benjamin Caunt, or the works commissioner Sir Benjamin Hall, who supervised installation.

Walk across **Westminster Bridge** to the south bank of the river for the best views of the Houses of Parliament. Today this bridge (built in 1862) is one of over 30 across the Thames, but in 1750 the original bridge on this site was only the second crossing, built after London Bridge. As you walk across look at the water which, despite its murky appearance, supports over a hundred species of fish, including salmon – there have even been recent sightings of seals in the river.

On the bridge's south side turn left along the footpath beside the river. The huge building to your right is County Hall, once the seat of London's metropolitan council. It now houses a hotel, restaurants, the **London Aquarium** (➤ 104), The **Dali**

Universe (► 103) and the ticket office for the **British Airways London Eye** (► 104), a massive wheel from whose slow-moving capsules you get spectacular views of the city. Look across the river from here for dramatic views of modern Charing Cross station.

Continue on past the somewhat drab concrete buildings of the **South Bank Centre**, one of the city's main cultural and arts venues (► 105 and 110).

Climb the steps up on to **Waterloo Bridge** for one of the finest views of London. Looking east, the dominant landmarks are St. Paul's Cathedral (► 78– 81), St. Bride's Church spire, Tower 42 (formerly the NatWest Tower), Lloyd's Building (► 173) and – in the far distance – Canary Wharf. In the near distance, on the right, stands the Oxo Tower (► 105).

As you walk to the north side of the bridge, the grand building just to the right is Somerset House, the only remaining example of the 18th-century mansions that once lined the Strand. It now houses three world-class collections (► 85).

Walk down the steps on to Victoria Embankment on the river's north bank. The road is busy and noisy, but you can look back to the south bank from here and there are plenty of seats *en route* to Westminster. You also pass Cleopatra's Needle, an 59-feet-high Egyptian obelisk dating from 1475 BC, given to Britain in 1819 by the Viceroy of Egypt.

Near Westminster Bridge stop at Westminster Pier to check on the times, prices and destinations of the river trips (► 102–103) available.

TAKING A BREAK

Try the Royal Festival Hall's bar, buffet lunch area and coffee shop, or stop for a pre-theater meal at the **People's Palace** (► 109).

⑪ Tate Modern

Britain's newest art museum, housed in a strikingly converted power station right in the center of the rejuvenated South Bank, was greeted with universal acclaim when it opened in May 2000. The gallery encompasses the spectrum of modern art movements from 19th-century Impressionism to the challenging work of young British artists of the late 20th and early 21st centuries.

Once inside, many visitors find the scale of the Turbine Hall, which occupies the bulk of the building, amazing: it resembles a vast, vacant cathedral, measuring 525 feet in length and 115 feet in height. This space is partly filled by works especially commissioned for the venue.

The **permanent collection** is exhibited on Levels 3 and 5. Each level is divided into two: the east end of **Level 3**, devoted to "Still Life/Object/Real Life," is the place to begin. It opens conventionally enough with Cezanne's *Still Life with Water Jug* but soon becomes more challenging. Salvador Dali's *Lobster Telephone* is in the room titled "Subversive Objects," while Peter Fischli and David Weisse have created a gallery of clutter – boards stacked carelessly, an empty yogurt carton, cigarettes and paint-spattered boots – that resembles work in progress. The west side of Level 3 is allotted to "Landscape/Matter/ Environment," with a whole room devoted to Mark Rothko's *Seagram Murals* – massive Abstract Expressionist works in maroon and black.

The eastern half of **Level 5** is titled "Nude/Action/Body." It starts with a dynamic Rodin sculpture, *The Kiss*, and goes on with work by Henri Matisse and Francis Bacon. To the west, "History/Memory/Society" is a highlight for many, with Picasso's *Weeping Woman* and Warhol's multiple images of Marilyn Monroe in *Marilyn Diptych*.

For many visitors, the views of London afforded from the upper floors of the gallery are as exciting as the works of art. From the East Room of **Level 7**, there is a superb panorama north across the river, over the Millennium Bridge to St. Paul's Cathedral. The view from the east window looks down upon Shakespeare's Globe (➤ 106) and spreads across toward

Above: The dramatic Turbine Hall

Docklands. From the south window, you can look across to the London Eye (► 104).

TAKING A BREAK

The **Globe Café** (► 108), a short distance from Tate Modern, serves light lunch dishes. The museum's top-floor restaurant is also good and enjoys spectacular views over the Thames.

Below: Jackson Pollock's lively *Summertime*, one of the works on display

🚇 201 E3 ✉ Bankside, SE1 ☎ 020 7887 8000; www.tate.org.uk 🕐 Daily 10–6 (also 6–10 pm Fri–Sat) 🚇 Southwark 🚇 Waterloo (East), Blackfriars, London Bridge 💷 Free; admission charge for special exhibitions on Level 4

TATE MODERN: INSIDE INFO

Top tips To avoid the crush, visit on weekday mornings or take advantage of the late opening on Fridays and Saturdays – by 8:30 pm the crowds tend to thin out.

• Self-guiding audio-tours are available, but the **free daily guided tours** (usually commencing at 10:30 am) are more engaging.

• **Photography** is allowed only in the Turbine Hall.

• Once it is reopened, the **Millennium Bridge**, linking St. Paul's Cathedral to Tate Modern, will be the best way to approach the gallery, taking visitors across the Thames and straight into its heart. Work continues on the bridge, which proved unstable in high wind and was closed to the public.

At Your Leisure

❶ Tate Britain

Until 2000, this Millbank gallery housed the Tate's entire collection, though limited gallery space meant that only a fraction of the works were on display at any one time. The solution was simple: divide the collection between two sites. Since the creation of Tate Modern (▶ 100–101), the gallery space has been refurbished and expanded. Both critics and general public seem delighted with the results.

Tate Britain covers five centuries of British art, from *A Man in a Black Cap* by John Bettes (1545), to work by latter-day British painters David Hockney, Francis Bacon, Lucian Freud, Stanley Spencer and sculptures by Henry Moore and Jacob Epstein.

All the paintings at Tate Britain are periodically rehung and sometimes disappear into storage for lack of space – though since the split this is much less of a problem. During any visit, however, you can count on seeing great works by Hogarth, Reynolds, Gainsborough, Constable and, of course, J. M. W. Turner. Turner is regarded as the greatest homegrown

Ophelia by John Everett Millais, one of Tate Britain's popular Pre-Raphaelite works

talent and has his very own wing, the Clore Gallery. But many visitors' favorites are still the impossibly romantic works of the late 19th-century Pre-Raphaelites – principally John Everett Millais, William Holman Hunt and, in particular, Dante Gabriel Rossetti. Look out for Millais's *Ophelia*, Rossetti's *Beata Beatrix* and *The Lady of Shalott* by John William Waterhouse.

✚ 199 F2 ✉ Millbank SW1 ☎ 020 7887 8000; www.tate.org.uk ⊙ Daily 10–5:50; closed Dec 24–26 🍴 Café, espresso bar and restaurant ⊜ Pimlico 🚌 2, 36, 88, 77A, C10, 185 💲 Expensive

❹ River Trips

A trip along the Thames is a tremendous way to see the city, away from the Underground or traffic-clogged streets. Piers in central London from which you can take trips are Westminster, Charing Cross/Embankment, Temple and the Tower of London. Services east to Greenwich (with connections out to the Thames Barrier) pass through a largely urban and industrial landscape, but offer excellent views of Greenwich (► 176–179). Services upstream to Hampton Court via Kew (► 162–163), Putney, Richmond and on to Kingston are more rural, the river meandering through parks and alongside some of London's more village-like residential enclaves. An evening cruise is also a lovely way to see the city, the river banks enlivened by the twinkling and gleaming of a million lights. Note that timetables vary from month to month, so be sure to go to the piers or telephone for latest details.

Frog Tours

London's most novel river ride is aboard a yellow amphibious ex-World War II DUKW vehicle, operated by Frog Tours. It begins on dry land, from County Hall, tours various central London landmarks, then returns to Vauxhall to splash down into the Thames and cruise the river for 30 to 35 minutes. It's expensive but fun. Advance booking is essential, tel: 020 7928 3132

From Westminster Pier

Upriver to Kew (1½ hours), Richmond (3 hours) and Hampton Court (4½ hours) tel: 020 7930 2062 or 020 7930 4721.
Downriver to Tower Pier (30 min) and Greenwich (1 hour) tel: 020 7237 5134.

From Embankment Pier

Downriver to Greenwich (1 hour) and Circular Cruise (50 min) nonstop to Houses of Parliament/Tower Bridge tel: 020 7987 1185.

From Tower Pier

Upriver to Westminster (30 min) tel: 020 7515 1415 and Embankment (25 min) tel: 020 7987 1185.
Downriver to Greenwich (30–40 min) tel: 020 7987 1185.
Evening cruises On an evening dinner cruise (3 hours) you can sightsee while wining and dining. Woods River Cruises operate three times weekly tel: 020 7480 7770 and the London Showboat two to three times per week, tel: 020 7237 5134.

⑤ Dalí Universe

As you wander into this surreal space and read on the walls such epigrams as "To be a real Dalinian one must first be a real masochist" and "There is less madness to my method than there is method to my madness," you begin to get some idea of what is in store. The most notable of the 500-plus exhibits are the sculptures – the largest collection of such in the world. Many of these are eye-popping, such as the disturbingly dislocated *Space Venus* (a copy of which stands outside) and will entertain seasoned Dalí watchers and first-timers alike. Look out for the famous Mae West red lips sofa and beautiful glass sculptures of Dalí's trademark soft watches (though note that Dalí's most famous paintings are elsewhere).

✚ 200 B1 ✉ County Hall, Riverside Buildings, SE1 ☎ 020 7620 2720
🕙 Daily 10–5:30 (last admission)
🍴 Café 🚇 Westminster, Waterloo
🚌 1, 4, 26, 59, 68, 76, 77,168, 171, 172, 176, 188, 211, 243, 341, 381, 501, 507, 521, X68 💷 Expensive

Marine marvels at the London Aquarium

⑥ London Aquarium

Even if the sight of fish behind glass usually leaves you cold, you are likely to be captivated by this modern aquarium. Its centerpiece is a huge glass tank, several stories high, in which all manner of sea life swims serenely past as visitors spiral down wide walkways and gaze in from all levels. There is something mesmeric about the apparently gentle glide of the sharks, the sheer ugliness of the gigantic eels and the bottom-hugging immobility of the giant rays. Smaller surrounding tanks are devoted to different watery environments, and there's an open tank full of rays for visitors to stroke.

🚇 200 B1 ✉ County Hall, Westminster Bridge Road, SE1 ☎ 020 7967 8007 🕐 Daily 10–6:30 🍴 Café 🚇 Westminster, Waterloo 🚌 12, 53, 76, 109, 171A, 211, P11 💲 Expensive

⑦ British Airways London Eye

The London Eye has proved to be one of the most successful of the capital's Millennium projects, and although it was intended as a temporary structure, few Londoners expect it to be taken down in 2005.

At 443 feet in diameter, the wheel is the biggest of its kind in the world, and as the 32 glass capsules are fixed on the outside of the wheel (rather than hung from it), you can enjoy totally unobstructed views over the city. On a clear day you can see as far as 25 miles, though the views immediately below and of the wheel itself are the most arresting. The capsules easily accommodate their maximum load of 25 passengers and give almost total all-round visibility, so there's no scrambling for the best view.

The Eye is in constant motion, revolving less than one inch per second, and it takes 30 minutes for a full revolution.

At busy times, it is essential to make a reservation by telephone or in person. Even then, you face a line of 30 minutes or so before boarding.

🚇 200 B2 ✉ County Hall Riverside Buildings ☎ Ticket hotline 0870 500 0600 (small booking charge); www.ba-londoneye.com 🕐 Daily 10–6, Nov–Mar, 9 am–late evening, Apr–Oct. Closed part Feb for annual maintenance 🍴 Cafés outside and in booking area 🚇 Westminster or Waterloo 🚌 1, 4, 26, 59, 68, 76, 77,168, 171, 172, 176, 188, 211, 243, 341, 381, 501, 507, 521, X68 💲 Expensive

⑧ Imperial War Museum

This fascinating, but sobering museum is much more than a display of military might or a glorification of war – despite the name, the monstrous guns in the forecourt and the militaristic slant of the vehicles on show in the main hall. The museum's real emphasis and strengths are the way in which it focuses on the effects of war in the 20th century on the lives of military personnel and civilians alike. This is achieved through a comprehensive col-

Tallest in London
- Canary Wharf Tower 797 feet
- Tower 42 (formerly the NatWest Tower) 604 feet
- Telecom Tower 577 feet
- British Airways London Eye 443 feet
- Nelson's Column 174 feet

lection of artifacts, documents, photographs, works of art, and sound and film archive footage. Some of the most moving testimonies come from oral descriptions recorded by ordinary people whose lives were deeply affected by their wartime experiences. For those who have never experienced war at first hand, this is the place to deepen your understanding.

🔲 Off map 200 C1 ✉ Lambeth Road, SE1
☎ 020 7416 5320; www.iwm.org.uk ⏰ Daily
10–6; closed Dec 24–26 🍴 Café
🚇 Lambeth North, Elephant and Castle,
Waterloo 🚌 1, 12, 45, 53, 63, 68, 168, 171,
172, 176, 188, 344 💰 Free

9 South Bank Centre

The vibrant South Bank arts complex is crammed with theaters, concert halls, movie theaters, bars, a gallery and restaurants. Though architecturally austere, on a warm summer's day it can still be a pleasant spot in which to relax. There is a genuine buzz, thanks to the crowds of people drawn to the complex's restaurants and cafés, and the (often free) concerts and exhibitions held in the

Fighter planes and rockets in the Imperial War Museum's main hall

major lobbies. A program of redevelopment, beginning in 2002 with a refurbishment of the Royal Festival Hall, is set to give the complex a complete makeover. In 2004, the acclaimed Museum of the Moving Image reopens in new premises close to the Royal Festival Hall. For more information on ticket reservations for productions at one of the South Bank Centre's theaters ► 110.

🔲 200 C2 🚇 Waterloo
🚌 Waterloo Bridge 1, 4, 26, 59, 68, 76, 77, 168, 171, 172, 176, 188 211, 243, 341, 381, 501, 507, 521, X68

10 Oxo Tower

This landmark building houses a dynamic mixture of private and public housing, restaurants and bars (► 109), designer workshops and the intriguingly titled Museum Of, which stages eclectic temporary exhibitions. The tower's windows are carefully placed to spell out the word "OXO" (a brand of stock cube), a clever ploy by the architect to evade regulations against riverside advertising. It's worth a visit for the superb views from the observation area alone.

➕ 201 D3 ✉ Barge House Street, SE1
☎ Museum Of: 020 7401 2255
🕐 Observation area, Level 8: daily 11–10; studios and shops Tue–Sun 11–6; Museum Of: Wed–Sun noon–6:30
🚇 Blackfriars, Waterloo 🚌 45, 63, 100, 381 ♿ Free all areas

The project was the brainchild of Sam Wanamaker, the American movie actor and director, who died before its completion. His legacy is an extraordinary achievement, not least because the theater itself is a wonderfully intimate and atmospheric space. It is built of unseasoned oak held together with 9,500 oak pegs, topped by the first thatched roof completed in the city since the Great Fire of London in 1666. It is also partly open to the

🄓 Shakespeare's Globe

How about a visit to Shakespeare's theater? Well, almost: this is a reconstruction of the Globe Theatre (whose original site lay about 300 yards away) in which Shakespeare was an actor and shareholder, and in which many of his greatest plays were first performed.

The Globe is a faithful re-creation of Shakespeare's original Elizabethan theater

elements, as was Shakespeare's original Globe, with standing room in front of the stage where theater-goers can heckle the actors in true Elizabethan fashion.

A visit to the exhibition and a tour of the theater is highly worthwhile and will certainly whet your appetite for a performance. The tours cover the history of the project, future plans

and costumes from past productions.

➕ 201 E3 ✉ New Globe Walk, Bankside, SE1 ☎ 020 7902 1500; box office 020 7401 9919; www.shakespeares-globe.org ⓘ Exhibition and tours: daily 9–4 (last tour noon), May–Sep; 10–5, Oct–Apr 🍴 Coffee bar, café and restaurant Ⓜ Mansion House, London Bridge, Cannon Street 🚌 Blackfriars Bridge 45, 63, 100; Southwark Street 344, 381 💷 Moderate

🔢 Vinopolis

If your idea of a good museum is the sort of place where you can saunter about with a glass of fine wine in your hand then you will enjoy Vinopolis. Set in historic vaults, which were once at the center of Europe's wine trade, this new award-winning attraction takes visitors on an encyclopedic trawl through the world of wine, visiting every major wine-producing country and region, assisted by tutored tastings, touch-screen technology and audio-guides. There's a super wine, food and accessories store, plus an excellent restaurant and wine bar.

➕ 201 F3 ✉ 1 Bank End, Bankside SE1 ☎ 0870 4444 777; www.vinopolis.co.uk ⓘ Mon 11–9, Sun, Tue–Fri 11–6, Sat 11–8 🍴 Restaurant, wine bar Ⓜ London Bridge 🚌 Blackfriars Bridge 45, 63, 100; Southwark Street 381, 344 💷 Expensive (includes wine tasting)

🔢 HMS *Belfast*

This World War II vessel, the biggest cruiser ever built by the Royal Navy, took part in the Normandy landings, and remained in service until 1965. Preserved in the state it enjoyed during active service, the ship is now moored between Tower Bridge and London Bridge on the south side of the Thames. It houses displays connected with recent Royal Navy history, but the ship itself remains the true attraction. You can explore all the

HMS *Belfast*, high seas warrior until 1965

way from the bridge to engine and boiler rooms nine decks below, taking in the cramped quarters of the officers and crew, the galleys, punishment cells and sick bays, as well as the gun turrets, magazines and shell rooms.

➕ 202 B2 ✉ Moored off Morgans Lane, Tooley Street, SE1 ☎ 020 7940 6300; www.hmsbelfast.org.uk ⓘ Daily 10–6, Mar–Oct (last admission 5:15); 10–5, Nov–Feb (last admission 4:15). Closed 24–26 Dec 🍴 Many nearby in Hay's Galleria (➤ 110) Ⓜ London Bridge, Tower Hill, Monument 🚌 42, 47, 78, 188, 381 💷 Moderate; free for children age 15 or under

For Kids

- London Aquarium (➤ 104)
- Boat trip downriver or on the Frog Tour (➤ 102–103)
- London Eye (➤ 104)
- HMS *Belfast* (➤ 107)

Where to...
Eat and Drink

Prices

Expect to pay per person for a meal excluding drinks and service

$ under £25 $$ £25–£50 $$$ over £50

Bengal Clipper $$

A former cardamom warehouse, next to the Conran Gastrodome at Butler's Wharf, makes a particularly fitting setting for this respected Indian restaurant. The spacious dining room is dominated by a central grand piano, the surroundings have a strong sense of style and comfort, and the service is elegant. The short menu specializes in mainly Bengal and Goan dishes.

➕ 202 F2 ⊠ Butler's Wharf, SE1
☎ 020 7357 9001; fax: 020 7357 9002
⊗ Lunch: daily noon–3 (also Sun 3–4). Dinner: Mon–Sat 6–11:30, Sun 6–11 ⊜ London Bridge, Tower Hill

Cantina del Ponte $–$$

This simple Italian-style eaterie, set on the riverside by Tower Bridge, has fabulous views back over the City. It is the least expensive of the Conran Gastrodome restaurants and the mainly Italian-inspired menu brings a simple choice of grilled or roasted meats and fish. In summer, ask for a table on the terrace backing on to the River Walk.

➕ 202 F2 ⊠ Butler's Wharf Building, 36c Shad Thames, SE1 ☎ 020 7403 5403; fax: 020 7403 0267 ⊗ Lunch: daily noon–2:45 (also Sat–Sun 12:45–3). Dinner Mon–Sat 6–10.45, Sun 6–9.45 ⊜ London Bridge, Tower Hill

sour (whisky with lemon). Otherwise the rest of the cooking is bulked out with beans and potatoes.

➕ 202 D2 ⊠ 150–152 Tooley Street, SE1 ☎ 020 7403 1342 ⊗ Lunch: Mon–Fri noon–3. Dinner: Mon–Sat 6:30–10 ⊜ London Bridge

The Circle Bar Restaurant $–$$

The Circle is one of a collection of fashionable eateries to be found at Butler's Wharf. The unusual layout features a restaurant set on a balconied mezzanine, which in turn overlooks the popular bar (where informal snacks are available).

There's a definite buzz, and the kitchen copes well with the mix of styles dictated by the globally influenced menu.

➕ 202 F2 ⊠ The Circle, 13–15 Queen Elizabeth Street, SE1 ☎ 020 7407 1122; fax: 020 7407 0123 ⊗ noon–10 ⊜ London Bridge, Tower Hill

Fina Estampa $

The capital's only Peruvian restaurant is set not far from London Bridge. The cooking is authentic and good value, the surroundings kitsch, but as peaceful as you can get with traffic rushing by. Shellfish is excellent, as is the *ceviche* (marinated raw fish), and it should all be washed down with a *pisco*

Globe Café $

There are stunning river views from the Georgian building that forms part of the Shakespeare's Globe theater complex on the South Bank. This airy, bright café serves light lunch and supper dishes such as pasta and salads, as well as cakes and sandwiches. The grill/restaurant on the second floor has the same river views, and offers an a la carte menu as well as good-value pre- and post-theater menus.

➕ 201 F3 ⊠ New Globe Walk, Bankside, SE1 ☎ 020 7902 1576, 020 7925 9444 ⊗ Café: Mon 10–6, Tue–Sun 10 am–11 pm. Restaurant: daily noon–3, 5:30–11 (closed Mon pm) ⊜ Cannon Street, London Bridge, Mansion House

Konditor & Cook $

Bright colors, plate-glass windows, and aluminum furniture characterize this ultra-modern café close to Waterloo train station. Open from breakfast through to dinner, the café serves a varied menu, with classics such as scrambled eggs and smoked salmon as well as Californian-Italian pasta dishes. The delicious cakes, made by their own bakery, are hard to resist, and the superb bread is baked on the premises too. Coffee is excellent.

➕ 201 D2 ☒ Young Vic, 66 The Cut, SE1 ☎ 020 7620 2700 ⏰ Mon–Fri 8:30 am–11 pm, Sat 10:30 am–11 pm Ⓔ Waterloo

Livebait $$

The menu at this informal and slightly cramped seafood restaurant incorporates traditional dishes such as rock and native oysters, cock crabs from Poole, and langoustines with mayonnaise. Added to this are a selection of interesting dishes that reflect Asian, oriental and

Mediterranean influences (often on the same plate). Close to the Old Vic and South Bank Centre.

➕ 201 D2 ☒ 43 The Cut, SE1 ☎ 020 7928 7211; fax: 020 7928 2279 ⏰ Mon–Sat noon–3, 5:30–11:30 Ⓔ Waterloo

Oxo Tower $$–$$$

Be warned; the Oxo Tower may be a Thames-side landmark but it can be hard to find. However, the elevator that expresses you to the 8th floor brings ample reward in stunning river vistas taking in St. Paul's and the Houses of Parliament. Window tables are not essential, as the view dominates the entire ultrachic space. Dishes are drawn from a global melting pot of influences, but in the evening there are more classic interpretations of European cooking.

➕ 201 D3 ☒ 8th Floor, OXO Tower Wharf, Barge House Street, SE1 ☎ 020 7803 3888; fax: 020 7803 3812 ⏰ Lunch: daily noon–2:30 (also Sun 2:30–4). Dinner: Mon–Sat 5:30–11, Sun 6–10 Ⓔ Blackfriars

People's Palace $$

This restaurant runs along the entire frontage of the Royal Festival Hall and is very convenient for the South Bank theaters and concert halls. The best seats are those by the windows overlooking the Thames, so book early. The cooking is fashionable, with strong Mediterranean and Asian accents. Pre-theater dinners are excellent value with ultra-efficient service.

➕ 200 B2 ☒ Level 3, Royal Festival Hall, Belvedere Road, SE1 ☎ 020 7928 9999; fax: 020 7928 2355 ⏰ Daily noon–3, 5:30–10:50 Ⓔ Waterloo

RSJ $$

The name RSJ refers to the steel joist that crosses the ceiling of this long-established family-owned restaurant. Among its numerous charms are a comfortably warm but contemporary interior, good, modern Anglo-French cooking strong on seasonal ingredients, great vegetarian dishes, and a much

applauded wine list. The set-price lunch is excellent value should you be heading for a matinee at the Royal National Theatre. Highly recommended.

➕ 200 C2 ☒ 13a Coin Street, SE1 ☎ 020 7633 0881; fax: 020 7401 2455 ⏰ Lunch: Mon–Fri noon–3. Dinner: Mon–Sat 5:30–11 Ⓔ Waterloo

Tas Restaurant $

In a street that is fast filling up with places to eat, Tas has something different to offer with its Turkish food and choice of *mezze*. The restaurant is large and brightly lit, with pale wooden tables and flooring and an open kitchen at the back; the chatter and hubbub create a definite buzz. Main courses are served in very generous portions and represent excellent value for money. The wine list is reasonable, with Turkish house wines.

➕ 201 D2 ☒ 33 The Cut SE1 ☎ 020 7928 1444 ⏰ Daily noon–11:30 Ⓔ Waterloo

Where to...
Shop

Borough Market (open: Mon–Sat 5:30–noon. Tube: London Bridge), at the junction of Borough High Street and Southwark Street, sells fruit and vegetables. Though there has been a market on this site since the 13th century, current threats of development mean that it is facing extinction. It's worth a visit if only to glimpse one of the few truly Dickensian areas left in London.

Hay's Galleria, opening on to the River Walk by the Thames (Tube: London Bridge), was one of the first warehouse developments. An impressive Victorian-style iron-and-glass roof covers a huge atrium that is surrounded by a mixture of offices, stores and cafés. The Galleria is noted for some quirky shops, but during the week the stores and eateries tend to cater to the needs of office workers. Though not worth a detour in itself, Hay's Galleria provides a pleasant watering hole if you are looking for a respite from some of the nearby attractions.

Gabriel's Wharf (Upper Ground, SE1. Tube: Waterloo), by Waterloo Bridge, close to the South Bank Centre, is a great place to buy unusual gifts. The lively complex contains design and craft workshops, where silversmiths and ceramicists sell their work, as well as several cafés. In summer a number of open-air events create a lively atmosphere.

The **Riverside Walk Market,** which sells secondhand books, is set up on the wide, paved space by the Thames under Waterloo Bridge every weekend between 10 am and 5 pm, and irregularly during the week. The stands stock mostly old paperbacks, but there are a few gems, including children's books, plays, poetry, science fiction and old map prints, to be found if you persevere.

Where to...
Be Entertained

FILM AND THEATER

Within the **South Bank Centre** (tel: 020 7960 4242. Tube Waterloo) are three venues, all of which stage music and dance events: **Royal Festival Hall (RFH1)** , the **RFH2,** (formerly the Queen Elizabeth Hall) and **RFH3** (formerly the Purcell Room). The complex is also home to **The Royal National Theatre** (Lyttelton, Olivier and Cottesloe theaters) and **National Film Theatre** (tel: 020 7928 3232), showing both subtitled foreign movies and mainstream releases. A major restoration project to improve the complex is underway.

The retrospectives and exhibitions of contemporary art, painting, sculpture and photography at the **Hayward Gallery** (Belvedere Road, SE1, tel: 020 7960 4242. Tube: Waterloo) are a must for art lovers.

Visit the **British Film Institute London IMAX Cinema** (1 Charlie Chaplin Walk, SE1, tel: 020 7902 1234. Tube: Waterloo) and see 3D movies on the largest screen in Europe.

CLUBS

Try the cutting-edge **Ministry of Sound** (103 Gaunt Street, SE1, tel: 020 7378 6528. Tube: Elephant and Castle). As with many London clubs, MoS plays different music on different nights (with dress codes in operation), so check listings magazines in advance for details (▶ 43). This is one of London's best-known clubs and an evening here won't be a budget outing.

Knightsbridge, Kensington and Chelsea

Getting Your Bearings

Ladbroke Grove
(800m)

9 **Portobello Road
Market**

Bayswater

Queensway

Notting Hill
Gate

BAYSWATER
ROAD

NOTTING HILL GATE

PEMBRIDGE ROAD

PORTOBELLO ROAD

KENSINGTON PARK ROAD

PALACE GDNS TERRACE

INVERNESS TERR

QUEENSWAY

LEINSTER TERR

8
**Kensington
Gardens**

THE BROAD WALK

These premier
residential
districts were once
leafy villages,
favored by the
wealthy for their
healthy distance from
the dirt and pollution of
early London. Today they
still retain an ambience of
exclusivity: Their houses are
grand, the streets still leafy,
and the area has attracted
many consulates and embassies
to its genteel environs.

KENSINGTON CHURCH STREET

Kensington
Palace **7**

Round
Pond

KENSINGTON ROAD

KENSINGTON HIGH ST

PALACE GATE

GLOUCESTER RD

High Street
Kensington

Kensington first gained its fashionable
reputation in the late 17th century when
royalty moved to Kensington Palace. The palace
remains a royal home – though parts are open to the public –
and the gardens are among London's prettiest. Kensington
Gardens occupies the western swathe of Hyde Park, which
extends all the way to Marble Arch, affording a magnificent
green space at the very heart of the city. In the middle is the
Serpentine, an artificial lake.

Much of Kensington is scattered with monuments to Queen
Victoria's husband, Prince Albert, who died at the age of 41. The
Albert Memorial on the edge of Kensington Gardens is the principal example, but more subtle reminders of the royal consort
survive elsewhere. It was the Prince's idea that profits from the
Great Exhibition (held in Hyde Park in 1851) should be used to
establish an education center in the area. The many colleges and
institutions of South Kensington were the result, among them
three of the capital's foremost museums: the Victoria and Albert
Museum, the Science Museum and the Natural History Museum.

Knightsbridge is Kensington's neighbor to the east and, if
anything, is even more exclusive as a residential address. It also
has a smart commercial aspect, including the department store
Harrods. More affluent residents use it as a local store, but most
Londoners and tourists are content with a voyeuristic look at
the richness and variety of its stock, its lavish interiors, and the
tempting food halls.

**Previous page:
The decorative
frieze on the
Royal Albert
Hall depicts
the Triumph of
Arts and Letters**

★ **Don't Miss**

2 Harrods ► 116

3 Victoria and Albert Museum
► 117

4 Science Museum ► 121

5 Natural History Museum ► 124

7 Kensington Palace ► 127

BAYSWATER ROAD

Marble Arch

Marble Arch

Lancaster Gate

Speakers' Corner

PARK LANE

Italian Gardens

8 Hyde Park

The Long Water

PARK LANE

Serpentine Bridge

Serpentine Gallery

The Serpentine

Hyde Park Corner

Albert Memorial **6**

Knightsbridge Barracks

KENSINGTON GORE

KENSINGTON ROAD

KNIGHTSBRIDGE

Knightsbridge

Royal Albert Hall

EXHIBITION ROAD

BROMPTON ROAD

Harrods **2**

SLOANE STREET

Royal College of Music

Imperial College

Science Museum **4**

Victoria & Albert Museum **3**

BEAUCHAMP PLACE

PONT STREET

5 Natural History Museum

CROMWELL ROAD

THURLOE PLACE

BROMPTON RD

South Kensington

SLOANE SQUARE

Sloane Square

LWR SLOANE ST

At Your Leisure

1 Chelsea Physic Garden
► 129

6 Albert Memorial ► 129

8 Hyde Park and Kensington Gardens ► 130

9 Portobello Road Market
► 131

KING'S ROAD

ROYAL HOSPITAL ROAD

CHELSEA BRIDGE RD

Royal Hospital

National Army Museum

0 ———— 500 metres
0 ———— 500 yards

Chelsea Physic Garden **1**

CHELSEA EMBANKMENT

Thames

Ensure a relaxed start to your day by browsing or luxury shopping in Harrods before heading to South Kensington's three principal museums and a royal palace set in beautiful gardens.

Knightsbridge, Kensington and Chelsea in a Day

10:00 am

2 Harrods (➤ 116) is essential viewing even if you don't want to spend any money. Don't miss the food halls, the pet department, the exotic Egyptian Hall or the daily performance by bagpipers. Have a coffee in one of the many in-store cafés.

11:30 am

Wander along **Brompton Road**, lined with exclusive stores, to the Victoria and Albert Museum. Or, if you don't fancy the half-mile walk, catch a number 14, 74 or C1 bus, any of which will drop you near the museum. The other museums are across the road.

The **3 Victoria and Albert Museum** (➤ 117–120), the national museum of art and design, is filled with all manner of beautiful objects; the **5 Natural History Museum** (entrance hall, below, ➤ 124–126) covers the earth's flora, fauna and geology; and the **4 Science Museum** (➤ 121–123) investigates every imaginable aspect of science. The best approach is to choose one museum and give it a couple of hours – don't try to tackle too much in one go.

1:30 pm

Have a leisurely lunch in the area at one of the museum cafés or in a
patisserie or pub in nearby Brompton Road.

2:45 pm

Walk north up Exhibition Road, turn left into Kensington Gore to the Royal
Albert Hall and admire the 6 Albert Memorial opposite (➤ 129). If the weather
is good head into Kensington Gardens and across to the Round Pond and
Kensington Palace. Otherwise, buses number 9, 10 or 52 run toward
Kensington High Street along Kensington Gore; get off at the Broad Walk (it's
just a couple of stops along) and walk straight into the gardens near the palace.
(Note that in winter the last admission to Kensington Palace is at 4 pm.)

3:30 pm

Look around 7 Kensington Palace (➤ 127–128), which is less grand than
Buckingham Palace, but the sort of place where you can imagine people
actually living. The palace's royal dress collection is especially good.

5:00 pm

Have a break in the Orangery (➤ 133) and then enjoy an evening walk through
8 Kensington Gardens and into 8 Hyde Park (above, ➤ 130–131): you might
even take a row-boat out on the Serpentine as a finale to the afternoon.

② Harrods

Harrods is a London institution. It began life when Henry Charles Harrod, a grocer and tea merchant, opened a small store in 1849. Today it contains over 300 departments spread across seven floors, still striving to fulfil its motto *Omnia Omnibus Ubique* – all things, for all people, everywhere.

Harrods works hard to maintain its reputation as London's premier department store. Uniformed doormen (known as Green Men) patrol the entrances and if you are deemed to be dressed inappropriately you'll be refused entry. Rucksacks, leggings, shorts or revealing clothing are to be avoided.

The store's most popular departments are the cavernous first-floor **food halls**, resplendent with decorative tiles and vaulted ceilings, where cornucopian displays of fish, fruit and myriad other foodstuffs tempt shoppers. Handsomely packaged teas, coffees, cookies and jars bearing the distinctive Harrods logo are available: good for gifts or souvenirs, and an inexpensive way to acquire the trademark carrier bag!

Also worth a special look are the **Egyptian Hall**, complete with sphinxes (also on the first floor) and the **Egyptian Escalator** that carries you to the store's upper floors. One perennial favorite is the **pet department** (on the third floor), whose most publicized sale was a baby elephant in 1967; the store keeps smaller livestock these days.

During your visit, keep an ear open for the distinctive sound of bagpipes. The Harrods' bagpipers perform daily, usually in the late morning on the first floor, but telephone for details.

The Harrods experience isn't complete unless you come back after dark when the vast exterior is brilliantly illuminated with thousands of lights.

Harrods' food halls are the most famous of the store's 300 or more departments

TAKING A BREAK
Stop in the first-floor food halls at the **Harrods Famous Deli** for delicious salt beef bagels or smoked salmon on rye.

➕ 195 F2 ✉ 87–135 Brompton Road, SW1 ☎ 020 7730 1234; www.harrods.com 🕐 Mon–Sat 10–7 🍴 19 bars and restaurants including a deli, pizzeria, sushi bar and a pub (serving Harrods' own beer) 🚇 Knightsbridge 🚌 C1, 14, 74

3 Victoria and Albert Museum

The Victoria and Albert Museum (also known as the V&A), the national museum of art and design, was founded in 1852 with the aim of making art accessible, educating working people, and inspiring designers and manufacturers. One of Europe's great museums, its 6 miles of galleries are crammed with exquisite exhibits from across the world and across the centuries.

This is the sort of place where you want to take just about everything home: some Meissen, perhaps, a few Persian carpets, an Indian throne, or the Heneage Jewel once owned by Queen Elizabeth I. The range of objects is staggering – sculpture, ceramics, glass, furniture, metalwork, textiles, paintings, photography, prints, drawings, jewelry, costume and musical instruments. In addition to the wealth of beautiful works of art, the V&A also has the most peaceful atmosphere and most interesting store of all the major London museums.

Casts and copies from the Italian Renaissance – just a fraction of the many beautiful works in the Victoria and Albert Museum

✚ 195 E1 ✉ Cromwell Road, SW7 ☎ 020 7942 2000; www.vam.ac.uk
🕐 Daily 10–5:45; Wed and last Fri of month 10–10 (Henry Cole Wing 10–5:30); closed Dec 24–26 🚇 South Kensington
🚌 C1, 14, 74. 🎟 Free

One of many highlights in the **Medieval Treasury** is the Limoges enamel Becket Casket, dating from 1180. It is covered with images depicting the death of St. Thomas à Becket at the hands of four knights loyal to King Henry II, whom Becket had angered by refusing to let Church authority be compromised by the Crown. The casket reputedly contained a bloodstained scrap of fabric from the clothes St. Thomas was wearing at his death. Look out also for the early church vestments, especially the Butler-Bowden Cope, embellished with fine embroidery.

The **Nehru Gallery of Indian Art** features an excellent display of textiles and paintings, together with a variety of other interesting artifacts such as a white jade wine cup and thumb ring belonging to Shah Jehan (a 17th-century Mogul

Suggested Route

- Medieval Treasury
- Nehru Gallery of Indian Art
- Raphael Cartoons
- Dress Collection
- Morris, Gamble and Poynter Rooms
- Canon Photography Gallery
- Cast Rooms
- Silver Gallery
- Glass Gallery

emperor of India and the builder of the Taj Mahal). One of the museum's most idiosyncratic items is also here – Tipu's Tiger (1790), a life-size wooden automaton from Mysore that shows a tiger eating a man. A music box inside the tiger's body can reproduce the growls of the tiger and screams of the victim.

Tipu's Tiger, one of the museum's most popular exhibits, shows a tiger mauling a British soldier – complete with sound effects

The V&A's **Raphael Cartoons** were commissioned by Pope Leo X in 1515 as designs for tapestries to hang in the Sistine Chapel in the Vatican. The word cartoon properly refers to a full-size preparatory drawing for works in other media. Important works of art, they depict scenes from the lives of St. Peter and St. Paul.

The **Dress Collection** traces the development of men's, women's and children's clothing through the ages. One of the museum's most popular sections, it gives you a chance to smirk at the fashions of your forebears, admire the often sumptuous dresses of centuries past, or marvel at historical oddities such as the 5-feet-wide mantua, a formal dress worn by 18th-century women for ceremonial occasions. Clothes from designers such as Dior, Issey Miyake, Versace and Chanel represent modern fashion.

A thousand years of fashion – the V&A's collection of historic dress is a highlight of any visit

The **Morris, Gamble and Poynter Rooms** are named after and decorated in the styles of three leading 19th-century artists and designers; the hugely influential William Morris (1834–96), who designed furniture and textiles, among much else; James Gamble (1835–1919), who worked as part of the museum's design team and produced stained glass and ceramics for his room, and artist Edward Poynter (1836–1919). They retain their original function as public refreshment rooms, the V&A having been the first museum in the world to provide its patrons with such facilities. Their painted tiles, friezes, columns, quotations and glass windows provide plenty to admire as you sip your coffee. Look in particular for some of the quotations that form part of the decorative scheme.

Left: The Italian Rooms display remarkable examples of Renaissance art and craftsmanship

A selection of the museum's 300,000 photographic works is displayed in the **Canon Photography Gallery**, alongside two

changing displays. This is one of the few spaces devoted to photography in a major London museum.

The **Cast Rooms** contain some of the museum's largest exhibits. In the 19th century art students were less able to travel to study masterpieces at first hand and to aid them reproductions (often casts) were made of famous sculptures. The rooms are packed with statues, windows, pulpits and altars: Size was clearly of no concern – parts of Trajan's Column in Rome and the enormous Portico de la Gloria from Santiago de Compostela in Spain are both reproduced.

The Victoria and Albert Museum moved to its present home in 1857. Until 1899 it was known as the South Kensington Museum

The **Silver Gallery** traces the history of silver from the 14th century, with examples of every size, shape and provenance. Exhibits range from the dramatic 18th-century Macclesfield Wine Service, testimony to an era of grand living and extravagant entertaining, to the silver snuff box that King Charles II gave to Nell Gwynn, the most beautiful of his many mistresses. In the How Do We Know exhibit, you learn how to identify a forgery, and in the discovery area visitors are allowed to handle some of the pieces in the collection.

The sparkling **Glass Gallery** tells the story of glass from 2500 BC to the present day. Make a special point of seeing *The Luck of Edenhall*, a 13th-century Syrian vessel probably brought home by a crusader but said by legend to have been created by fairies. A fabulous example of modern glass design is provided by the balustrade up to the mezzanine floor, the work of the American glass artist Danny Lane.

TAKING A BREAK

Stop at **Emporio Armani Caffè** (191 Brompton Road, SW3, tel: 020 7823 8818), an elegant second-floor café where Armani-clad waiters serve delicious modern Italian food.

VICTORIA AND ALBERT MUSEUM: INSIDE INFO

Top tips Late view takes place on Wednesday evenings and the last Friday of the month, with certain galleries remaining open until 10 pm. A lecture is given each Wednesday (charge) and themed events are staged on Fridays. Admission to the galleries is free though some events may carry a separate charge.

Hidden gems Take time to see the office of Pittsburgh department store proprietor Edgar J. Kaufmann, designed by American architect Frank Lloyd Wright (1869–1959). It is the only example of Wright's work in Europe.
• The **John Constable Collection** is the world's largest collection of works by this leading 19th-century British landscape artist.

❹ Science Museum

Technophobes needn't be afraid of this museum: The science here is presented in a simple and user-friendly way, with plenty of child-pleasing hands-on displays and clever devices to make sense of complex and everyday items alike. The museum embraces all branches of pure and applied science from their beginnings to modern times, covering the ground with enormous visual panache and a real desire to communicate the excitement and vibrancy of science.

Great working engines from the Industrial Revolution are popular exhibits at the Science Museum

Be warned before you start, you can easily spend the whole day here and still not see everything. With the addition of the stunning new Wellcome Wing, and its attendant IMAX theater and space simulator ride, the Science Museum, always one of London's biggest and best museums, has taken on an even larger dimension. It is best to concentrate on just a couple of themed galleries interspersing these with fun areas such as the movie theater and rides. If

you have children, let them off the leash in the museum's acclaimed hands-on areas.

The best way to start your visit is by strolling through **Making the Modern World,** on the first floor. This dramatic gallery displays many icons and "firsts" of the modern age; from Stephenson's record-breaking 1829 locomotive, the *Rocket,* to the scorched and battered Apollo 10 Command Module that orbited the moon in May 1969 as a precursor to the lunar landings (for a full history of space flight head to the adjacent Space gallery). Many peoples' favorites, however, are the huge, hypnotically rotating mill engines that powered the Industrial Revolution and are still steamed for museum visitors.

🔢 195 E1   ✉ Exhibition Road, SW7
☎ 020 7942 4000; www.sciencemuseum.org.uk
⏱ Daily 10–6; closed Dec 24–26
🍴 Kiosk and café   🚇 South Kensington
🚌 14, 49, 70, 74, 345, C1   💷 Free

To enter the deep-neon-blue world of the **Wellcome Wing**, its three upper floors suspended almost magically in mid-air, is truly to walk into the future. Many of the exhibits in this part of the museum deal with cutting-edge technology, and just-breaking scientific stories are monitored here in real time. If the latest advances in medicine and nuclear physics sounds a bit too much like hard work, however, take a ride to Mars aboard the Virtual Voyages simulator, or for an even more exciting show, head to the top floor where the IMAX theater will astound you with images as tall as five double-decker buses, and suck you right into the screen. Films such as *Blue Planet* and *Solarmax* portray the universe and Earth as you

Above: A replica of the Apollo lunar module in the Making the Modern World gallery

have never seen them before, but for eye-popping state-of-the-art cinematic special effects take the kids to *Cyberworld 3D*.

There are so many other diverse galleries to explore – Food, Gas, Computers, Time, Chemical Industry, Marine Engineering, Photography, Health, Geophysics and Oceanography, to name just a few – that it is difficult to know where to head for next. Try to make time, however, for **Flight**, a fascinating display chronicling the history of manned flight from Montgolfier's balloons to supersonic engines. Historic airplanes duck and dive, slung from every available piece of ceiling, and high-level walkways get you right up into the air alongside these beautiful gleaming machines.

Below: Historic airplanes on show in the Flight Gallery

TAKING A BREAK

Despite its name, the **Deep Blue Café** is a high-quality waiter-service restaurant serving suitably up-to-the-minute meals in an open-plan setting from which you can gape at the $58 million Wellcome Wing. The Museum Café on the first floor sits right next to a splendid mill engine behemoth of the Industrial Revolution.

Detailed models and innumerable hands-on displays around the museum help to bring science to life

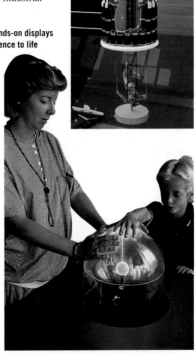

For Kids

The museum is committed to involving children and the four specialist galleries for them are all staffed by informative "Explainers."

- **The Garden** (basement): aimed at 3- to 6-year olds.
- **Things** (basement): aimed at 7- to 11-year olds.
- **Flight Lab** (fourth floor): explains the mysteries of flight.
- **Launch Pad** (basement): a range of scientific principles explained in a fun, hands-on environment.

On weekends and holidays access to these areas may be restricted and timed ticketing may operate. If this is the case tickets are allocated at the entrance to each gallery.

SCIENCE MUSEUM: INSIDE INFO

Top tips The **Launch Pad** (➤ For Kids panel, above) is particularly popular. To avoid the worst of the crowds, visit it either early or late in the day.

In more detail The **Science and Art of Medicine** (sixth floor) provides a fascinating and detailed history of medicine. It also looks at how different cultures interpret and treat illnesses. The range of items on display is remarkable, and includes old medical instruments, skulls, costumes, anatomical models and even shrunken heads.

- The **Secret Life of the Home** (in the basement) houses a fun collection illustrating how the everyday household items we take for granted have evolved and operate. There's also a set of household objects that never caught on – visitors are invited to guess their function.

5 Natural History Museum

The Natural History Museum has a staggering 69 million specimens, many (but not all) of which are on display. They cover lifeforms and the Earth's building blocks from the most distant past to the modern day. Everything in, under or on the Earth is here, the flora and fauna – from dinosaurs and whales to butterflies, humming birds and human beings – in the Life

Galleries, and the geological material in the Earth Galleries. Displays in both sets of galleries are entertaining and interactive – be warned, you could easily spend a whole day here.

Before you go in, take a look at the museum building, designed in the late 19th century in the style of a cathedral. Measuring some 656 feet from end to end, it was the first building in Britain to be wholly faced in terra-cotta.

The suggested route below will take about two hours. Alternately, the free museum plan has a useful breakdown of the museum's highlights.

The Natural History Museum is home to over 69 million exhibits

Life Galleries

The Wonders of the Natural History Museum (Gallery 10). This remarkable gallery is the entrance hall to the Life Galleries and contains a variety of breathtaking exhibits. The 94-feet-long cast of the fossilised skeleton of a Diplodocus dinosaur holds center stage, but the alcoves around the hall display remarkable items such as the fossilized egg of the Madagascan elephant bird (which is as big as a rugby ball). Follow the stairs to the fourth floor to see the section of a giant sequoia tree from San Francisco (giant sequoias are the largest living things on

---

✚ 195 D1 ✉ Cromwell Road, SW7 ☎ 020 7942 5000; www.nhm.ac.uk
🕐 Mon–Sat 10–5:50, Sun 11–5:50 (last admission 5:30); closed Dec 24–26
🍴 Cafés, restaurant, snack bar and fast-food restaurant
Ⓢ South Kensington 🚌 Near by 14, 49, 70, 74, 345, C1
♿ Free

Dinosaur skeletons are among the largest and most popular of the museum's exhibits. Of the 350,000 items that come to the museum every year, 250,000 are insect specimens

Special raised walkways bring you face to face with the likes of Tyrannosaurus Rex in the Dinosaur Gallery

the planet) and notice how the dates of major historical events have been marked in their appropriate place on the tree's "rings."

Dinosaurs (Gallery 21). The dramatic and popular displays here examine many aspects of most species of dinosaur, including some of the many theories as to why they became extinct. A raised walkway enables visitors to get close to the exhibits, and the exhibition includes a robotics display of dinosaurs in action.

Mammals (Galleries 23–4). Some of the material in these galleries consists of stuffed animals behind glass, and has been part of the museum for years. This said, the straightforward displays are almost a relief after the overwhelming variety of exhibits in other galleries: the model of the blue whale (92 feet long), in particular, is a perennial favorite.

Ecology (Gallery 32). This is one of the most visually impressive areas in the museum, with a striking mirrored video display of the Water Cycle, and a walk-in leaf to illustrate just how vital plants are to the life of the planet. It does a good job of explaining often complex ecological issues and the need for responsibility with regard to the environment.

Creepy Crawlies (Gallery 33). In this gallery devoted to bugs and beasties, you'll learn more than you ever wanted to know about insects, spiders, crustaceans and centipedes. It will leave you wondering just what lurks in your home; not for the squeamish.

Earth Galleries

Visions of Earth (Gallery 60). An escalator carries visitors away from the Earth Galleries' impressive entrance hall through a huge hollow earth sculpture into the upper galleries. It's a stunning introduction to this part of the museum, but before you go up examine the displays behind the tiny portholes in the walls: Many of the specimens on show here are beautifully shaped and have almost impossibly brilliant colors. Look out, in

The dramatic entrance to the Earth Galleries

particular, for the piece of moon rock and the ancient fossils that were once believed to have been the devil's toenail and the weapons of Zeus.

The Power Within (Gallery 61). This highly visual gallery seeks to explain volcanoes and earthquakes; its memorable centerpiece is a mock-up of a supermarket which simulates the 1995 Kobe earthquake in Japan which killed 6,000 people.

Earth's Treasury (Gallery 64). Such is the beauty and variety of the items on show, it takes a while to realize that what is on display is simply specimens of gems, rocks and minerals. Exhibits range from priceless diamonds, emeralds and sapphires to grains of sand: You'll never look at a humble rock in quite the same way again.

TAKING A BREAK

A fossil exhibit

Stop for lunch at either **Emporio Armani Caffè** (➤ 120) or **Deep Blue Café** (➤ 123), both on the Brompton Road.

NATURAL HISTORY MUSEUM: INSIDE INFO

Top tips The main museum entrance on Cromwell Road leads into the Life Galleries: the entrance in Exhibition Road takes you to the Earth Galleries. The two are joined by Gallery 50.

• The museum is **quietest** early or late on weekdays, but all periods during school holidays are busy.

• **Investigate** (Gallery B2) is a special children's discovery area.

7 Kensington Palace

Kensington Palace has been the home of various members of royalty for many centuries but came most prominently to public notice only when the late Diana, Princess of Wales moved here. This is an attractive and historic palace, well worth a visit for its setting, art treasures, State Rooms, fine furnishing and Royal Ceremonial Dress Collection.

Flowers are still left at the gates of the palace in memory of Diana, Princess of Wales

The mansion began life as a country house in 1605 but was converted into a palace by Sir Christopher Wren for King William III and Queen Mary II following their accession to the throne in 1689. Later resident monarchs included Queen Anne, George I and George II, while Queen Victoria was born, baptized and grew up in the palace. It was also here that she was woken one morning in June 1837 to be told that her uncle (William IV) had died and that she was Queen. Today, Princess Margaret, the Duke and Duchess of Gloucester and Prince and Princess Michael of Kent all have private apartments in the palace.

The south front of Kensington Palace was designed in 1695 by Nicholas Hawksmoor

Visits to the palace begin downstairs with the **Royal Ceremonial Dress Collection** and then move upstairs to the **State Apartments**. In the former, you can see the sumptuous clothes that would have been worn by those being presented at

🔲 194 B3 ✉ The Broad Walk, Kensington Gardens, W8
☎ 020 7937 9561; www.hrp.org.uk
🕐 Daily 10–5 (last entry) Apr–Oct; daily 10–4 (last entry) Nov–Mar.
🍴 Restaurant in the Orangery (➤ 133) serving light meals and snacks, afternoon tea
🚇 High Street Kensington, Queensway
🚌 9, 10, 12, 33, 49, 52, 52A, 94, C1
💷 Moderate

Top: The King's Gallery displays the palace's finest paintings

Above: The King's Staircase, with portraits of royal courtiers

court at the turn of the 19th century. For many visitors, the most interesting part of the exhibition are the dresses belonging to the late Diana, Princess of Wales.

Upstairs, the apartments of King William III and (less grand) rooms of his wife, Queen Mary II, have been restored to their 18th-century appearance. Their most impressive corner is the Cupola Room, decorated in the style of ancient Rome with an excess of gilded statues and classical painting: It was here that Queen Victoria's baptism took place in 1819. The room's centerpiece is an 18th-century clock called *The Temple of the Four Grand Monarchies of the World*, whose intricate decoration far outshines the tiny clockface itself.

The palace has seen its share of tragedy. Mary II succumbed to smallpox here at age 32 in 1694, and when Queen Anne's beloved husband, Prince George, died in 1708, she did not return to the palace for many months. Like Mary, she also died here six years later, at age 49, a sad figure who, despite 18 pregnancies, saw none of her children live beyond age 11. King George II ended his days here too – while on the toilet.

TAKING A BREAK

Enjoy a classic English afternoon tea in pleasant surroundings in the **Orangery** (➤ 133).

KENSINGTON PALACE: INSIDE INFO

Top tips Access to the palace is from the back of the building, from The Broad Walk in Kensington Gardens.
• Note there is **no official monument here to Diana**, Princess of Wales though people continue to bring flowers to the palace.
• Be sure to visit the **Orangery** (➤ 133), built for Queen Anne and now a restaurant, and don't miss the pretty **Sunken Garden**.

At Your Leisure

Chelsea Physic Garden

This small garden is a quiet corner of pretty, rural tranquillity in the heart of the city, with over 5,000 species of plants growing in attractive profusion. Established in 1673, it was founded by the Royal Society of Apothecaries to study medicinal plants, making it the oldest botanical garden in England after Oxford's. It also retains the country's oldest rockery (1773) and the first cedars in England were planted here in 1683. After green-seeded cotton plants from the Caribbean islands were nurtured in the garden, seed was sent to Georgia in the American colonies in 1732 and contributed to what would later develop into the huge cotton plantations of the South.

🔲 198 A1 ✉ Swan Walk, 66 Royal Hospital Road, SW3 ☎ 020 7352 5646; www.cpgarden.demon.net
🕐 Wed noon–5, Sun 2–6, Apr–Oct
Ⓜ Sloane Square 🚌 239
💷 Moderate

Albert Memorial

This gleaming memorial, is the most florid and exuberant of all London's monumental statues. It was completed in 1872 by Sir George Gilbert Scott, winner of a competition to design a national memorial to Prince Albert of Saxe-Coburg-Gotha (1819–61), Queen Victoria's husband, though it was not unveiled until four years later. Victoria and Albert married in 1840, but Albert died of typhoid aged just 41 years, a blow from which Victoria never quite recovered.

For Kids
- Science Museum (➤ 121–123)
- Natural History Museum (➤ 124–126)
- Boating on the Serpentine or feeding ducks in Kensington Gardens and Hyde Park (➤ 130–131)
- Harrods' toy department (➤ 116)

What Albert – who didn't want a memorial – would have made of the neo-Gothic pile is hard to imagine: his spectacular gilded statue is some three times life size, and the whole edifice rises 115 feet, its apex crowned with the figures of Faith, Hope and Charity. The figures around the edges portray subjects such as astronomy, poetry and sculpture, plus enterprises close to Albert's heart such as agriculture, manufacturing and commerce. The 169 sculptures around the base portray figures from history – there's not one woman among them – while those set slightly apart are allegories of the four continents: Europe, Africa, America and Asia.

🔲 195 D2 ✉ South Carriage Drive, Kensington Gardens, SW7 ☎ 020 7495 0916 for guided tours Ⓜ High Street Kensington, Knightsbridge 🚌 9, 10, 52

The Albert Memorial, restored to its original gilded glory

Above: Boats on the Serpentine in the rural haven of Hyde Park. Below: Sculpture by Henry Moore in Hyde Park

Map labels:
BAYSWATER ROAD
Marble Arch
Speakers Corner
BAYSWATER ROAD
Italian Gardens
8 Hyde Park
8 Kensington Gardens
The Long Water
Round Pond
Serpentine Bridge
Serpentine Gallery
The Serpentine
Albert Memorial 6
Knightsbridge Barracks
KENSINGTON GORE   KENSINGTON RD

🔠 Hyde Park and Kensington Gardens

Look at the map of London and you'll see a large swathe of green southwest of Marble Arch. Most of this is Hyde Park, but Kensington Gardens, formerly the grounds of Kensington Palace (➤ 127–128), occupies an area to the west of the Serpentine, the manmade lake at the park's heart.

Originally a tract of land set aside for Henry VIII to go hunting, **Hyde Park** was opened to the public in the early 17th century by James I, and today provides a magnificent and peaceful area in which to escape the city. **Speakers' Corner**, at its north-eastern edge near Marble Arch, is the place to air your views – anyone is entitled to stand up here and (within certain parameters) speak their mind: Sunday afternoons draw the most orators. Farther west stretches the **Serpentine**, an artificial lake created in 1730 by Caroline, queen to George II, for boating and bathing.

Above: Hyde Park's Speakers' Corner

It's now a good a place to while away an hour on the water – row-boats and peddle boats are available for rent on the northern bank. You can also swim at certain times in a designated area off the south shore.

The **Serpentine Gallery** at the heart of **Kensington Gardens** shows a changing program of modern and often controversial art throughout the year. Other art in the park includes a variety of statues, most famously that of Peter Pan (1912), the boy who never grew up, which was paid for by the story's author, J. M. Barrie, who lived nearby. It's just off a walkway on the Serpentine's west bank, near the lake's northern limit.

Hyde Park
➕ 195 E3 🕐 Daily 5 am–midnight
🚇 Hyde Park Corner, Knightsbridge, Lancaster Gate, Marble Arch

Kensington Gardens
➕ 194 C3 🕐 Daily 5 am–midnight
🚇 High Street Kensington, Bayswater, Queensway, Lancaster Gate

Serpentine Gallery
➕ 195 D3 ☎ 020 7402 6075 🕐 Daily 10–6 during exhibitions 🎟 Free

❾ Portobello Road Market

Portobello is London's largest market, the long street and its environs hosting a wide variety of food, modern clothing, crafts and junk markets, as well as the antiques and specialty small shops (and stands) that first made it famous. On Saturdays it is the scene of what is reputedly the world's largest antiques market, with over 1,500 traders, the majority of whom are located at the street's southern end after the intersection with Westbourne Grove. Fruit stands dominate beyond Elgin Crescent, while junk, second-hand clothes and more off-beat stores and stands take over beyond the "Westway" expressway overpass.

The range and quality of antiques and other goods is enormous. At the top end prices are as high as any in London, but bargains and one-offs can still be found; it's great fun to browse and people-watch even if you don't want to spend anything.

Note that on fine summer days the market is often extremely crowded (beware of pickpockets).

➕ 194 A4 🕐 Antiques: Sat 4–6. Clothes/bric-a-brac: Fri 7–4, Sat 8–5, Sun 9–4. General: Mon–Wed 8–6, Thu 9–1, Fri–Sat 7–7 🚇 Notting Hill Gate, Ladbroke Grove 🚌 23, 27, 28, 31, 52, 328

A colorful corner of Portobello Road

Where to...
Eat and Drink

Prices
Expect to pay per person for a meal excluding drinks and service
$ under £25 $$ £25–£50 $$$ over £50

The Ark $$
The clever use of mirrors has given extra depth to the narrow room at this revamped Kensington favorite. The menu includes a mixture of classic, modern and regional Italian favorites. Expect good *al dente* pasta, rustic meat dishes served with polenta, and a perfect grilled veal chop. An attractively priced lunch menu has proved immensely popular, and in the evening the menu expands and gains some specials.

🕂 194 B3 ⊠ 122 Palace Gardens Terrace W8 ☎ 020 7229 4024 🕐 Daily noon–3; 6:30–11 (closed Sun pm) 🚇 Notting Hill Gate

Bibendum $$–$$$
Sir Terence Conran opened this, his premier restaurant, in the acclaimed Michelin building in 1987. It is both relaxed and highly professional, and the magnificent dining room provides a great setting for some serious cooking. The wide range of classic European dishes on the menu are given a modern twist. The depth of the wine list is a real talking point.

🕂 Off map 195 E1 ⊠ Michelin House, 81 Fulham Road, SW3 ☎ 020 7581 5817; fax: 020 7823 7925 🕐 Lunch: Mon–Sat noon–2, Sun 12:30–2.30. Dinner: Mon–Sat 7–11, Sun 7–10 🚇 South Kensington

Bluebird $$
A flower shop, café, high-profile bar, kitchen shop and classy supermarket are all part of the experience at this fashionable high-volume eaterie. There is a great buzz from the smart restaurant. The menu is simply conceived, with dishes from the shellfish bar, rotisserie, and the large wood-fired brick oven where a wide variety of meats, fish, poultry and vegetables are cooked over different types of wood.

🕂 Off map 198 A2 ⊠ 350 Kings Road, SW3 ☎ 020 7559 1000; fax: 020 7559 1111 🕐 Mon–Sat 11–3.30, 6–10; Sun noon–4:30, 6–11 🚇 Sloane Square

Fifth Floor at Harvey Nichols $$
The Fifth Floor restaurant, on the top floor of the designer-label Harvey Nichols department store (▲ 134), forms part of a food lover's paradise that takes in a food hall, café and bar, even *kaiten zushi*

(a conveyor-belt sushi bar). The dining room is cool and chic, while the food incorporates imaginative Italian, Middle Eastern and oriental influences. Both the restaurant and bar can become crowded at peak times. Reservations are essential.

🕂 198 A4 ⊠ Harvey Nichols, Knightsbridge, SW1 ☎ 020 7235 5250; fax: 020 7823 2207 🕐 Lunch: Mon–Fri noon–3, Sat–Sun noon–3.30. Dinner: Mon–Sat 6–11:30 🚇 Knightsbridge

Gordon Ramsay Restaurant $$$
The former Glasgow Rangers soccer player took the fast track to the top of the catering profession, gaining experience along the way with some of London's premier chefs as well as in France, in the kitchens of Guy Savoy and Joël Robuchon. Installed at the former La Tante Claire (discreetly restyled), Gordon Ramsay enthrals customers with a rich, yet light style of haute cuisine. The best value – and the best way to sample the Ramsay style – is the set three-

course lunch. Reserving well in advance is essential.

🚇 198 A1 ☒ 68–69 Royal Hospital Road, SW3 ☎ 020 7352 4441; fax: 020 7352 3334 🕐 Mon–Fri noon–2:30, 6:45–11 🚇 Sloane Square

Hilaire $$

Chef/proprietor Bryan Webb has ensured that this is one of the great small restaurants of London. Whether you're in one of the curved windows of the first-floor dining room or in a cozy basement alcove, a meal here is always a civilized experience. Uncompromising standards in choice of ingredients and exact technique produce consistently memorable results from a kitchen that eschews fashion, but nevertheless provides some of the best modern British cooking in this part of London.

🚇 Off map 195 E1 ☒ 68 Old Brompton Road, SW7 ☎ 020 7584 8993; fax: 020 7581 2949 🕐 Lunch: Mon–Fri 12:15–2:30. Dinner: Mon–Sat 6:30–11:30 🚇 South Kensington

The Orangery $

The elegant, white, light Orangery provides a pleasant, informal setting for English afternoon tea. Three set teas are offered, the grandest including champagne, or you could just opt for a selection of delicious cakes and a pot of tea. Light lunches are available between noon and 2:30.

🚇 194 B3 ☒ Kensington Palace, Kensington Gardens, W8 ☎ 020 7376 0239 🕐 Daily 10–5, Oct–Easter; 10–6 Easter–Sep 🚇 High Street Kensington

La Tante Claire $$$

Pierre Koffmann has followed in the steps of top London chefs Nico Ladenis and Marco Pierre White in moving his restaurant into a grand London hotel. In Koffmann's case the move has come after over two decades, and relocating from his former Chelsea base to the quiet and elegant Berkeley Hotel in the heart of Knightsbridge has proved an immediate success. The menu has changed little, continuing to offer simple preparations of classic French cooking, much of it based on the culinary traditions of Koffmann's native Gascony.

🚇 198 B4 ☒ The Berkeley Hotel, Wilton Place, SW1 ☎ 020 7823 2003; fax: 020 7823 2001 🕐 Lunch: Mon–Fri 12:30–2. Dinner: Mon–Sat 7–11 pm 🚇 Knightsbridge, Hyde Park Corner

Zafferano $$

In an understated room, the plain walls, terra-cotta floor, comfortable chairs and closely set tables all contribute to an air of upscale informality. Chef/proprietor Giorgio Locatelli's cooking comes as a breath of fresh air, presenting Italian food with an understanding and flair that many more pretentious establishments have difficulty matching. Unclustered and simply conceived dishes based on the finest ingredients, exact technique and clear flavors are the driving force behind lunch and dinner menus. In this expensive part of London, a meal at Zafferano's is a positive bargain.

🚇 198 B3 ☒ 15 Lowndes Street, SW1 ☎ 020 7235 5800; fax: 020 7235 1971 🕐 Lunch: daily noon–2:30. Dinner: Mon–Sat 7–11, Sun 7–10:30 🚇 Knightsbridge

BARS

Boisdale $$

An astonishing range of single malt whiskies is available at London's premier malt whisky bar. Furnishings offer the odd spot of tartan to emphasise the Scottish theme. Despite the presence of a cigar bar, this is not in any way a male preserve. Indeed, it's a pleasant place, with an attractive courtyard, a cozy, dark, atmospheric bar, and an adjoining restaurant that specializes in Scottish dishes.

🚇 198 C3 ☒ 15 Eccleston Street, SW1 ☎ 020 7730 6922 🕐 Lunch: Mon–Fri noon–2:30. Dinner: Mon–Sat 7–10:30. Bar 2:30–7 🚇 Victoria

Where to... Shop

The streets of Knightsbridge, Kensington and Chelsea provide some of London's most blue-blooded shopping, with the sophisticated coexisting alongside the traditional. Many stores don't open until 10 am, generally closing at 6 pm (some later). On a Sunday this becomes noon to 5 pm in most instances. Late-night shopping in this neighborhood is Wednesday (Kensington High Street, Thursday) with stores generally adding an extra hour on to their usual closing times.

KNIGHTSBRIDGE

Harvey Nichols (109–125 Knightsbridge, SW1, tel: 020 7235 5000. Tube: Knightsbridge). Fashion addicts can indulge themselves on three floors of designer womenswear, two floors of menswear and a first floor given over to up-to-the-minute accessories such as Wolford hosiery, Dolce & Gabbana sunglasses and all manner of scarves, perfumes and cosmetics. Minimalist surroundings house an industrial steel-and-glass sixth-floor food emporium consisting of an opulent food hall, a sushi bar, a café, a bar and a restaurant.

Harrods, probably London's best-known department store, is a must on most tourist itineraries (▲116). The store is renowned for food, gifts and household items as well as high fashion.

SLOANE STREET

Sloane Street, bounded at its northern end by Knightsbridge Underground station and on its southern end by Sloane Square, is a serious showcase for international designers. Italy is represented by the romantic designs of **Alberta Ferretti** (205–206 Sloane Street, SW1, tel: 020 7235 2349. Tube: Knightsbridge) – gauzes and shimmering silks in a chandeliered setting; by that master of understated neutrality, **Armani** (37 Sloane Street, SW1, tel: 020 7235 6232. Tube: Knightsbridge); and by the funky uniformity of **Prada** (43–45 Sloane Street, SW1, tel: 020 7235 0008. Tube: Knightsbridge). Just around the corner, **Agent Provocateur** (16 Pont Street, SW1, tel: 020 7235 0229. Tube: Knightsbridge) sells top-quality lingerie.

If all the choice of high fashion sends you into a closet (or wallet) crisis, slip into the old-fashioned stationery sanctuary of **Smythson's** (135 Sloane Street, SW1, tel: 020 7730 5520. Tube: Sloane Square) to scoop up leather-bound diaries and notebooks (available at significantly lower prices than in comparable stores), along with perfect engraved writing paper and envelopes.

KENSINGTON HIGH STREET AND KENSINGTON CHURCH STREET

Kensington High Street might be less slick, but it is very long and has lots of useful stores clustered around the High Street Kensington Underground station, including a major branch of Marks & Spencer and the department store Barkers.

Running north, opposite Barkers, is Kensington Church Street (Tube: Kensington High Street). an antique-lover's dream, with a fabulous concentration of dealers. Works by important 19th- and early 20th-century designers such as William Morris and Pugin are for sale at **Haslam & Whiteway** (105 Kensington Church Street, W8, tel: 020 7229 1145). Early English ceramics, including Staffordshire figures and early Wedgwood pieces, are available at **Jonathan Horne** (66c Kensington Church Street, W8, tel: 020 7221 5658), and Cornish ware, Midwinter and Poole potteries are the specialty at **Richard Dennis**

(144 Kensington Church Street, W8, tel: 020 7727 2061). Both dealers can organize shipping, as can **John Jesse** (160 Kensington Church Street, W8, tel: 020 7229 0312), who stocks 20th-century design including art nouveau prints. Wherever you buy, don't forget to thoroughly inspect the goods, haggle (it is expected) and request a receipt with an accurate description of the item.

SOUTH KENSINGTON

Individual stores at the **Natural History Museum** (▶ 124–126), the **Science Museum** (▶ 121–123) and the **Victoria and Albert Museum** (▶ 117–120) stock all the educational lines that you might expect: pocket-money toys, dinosaurs and pretty minerals at the Natural History Museum; rockets and robots at the Science Museum. The museum stores, however, are also a good hunting ground for top-quality gifts for discerning adults.

The **Victoria and Albert Museum store** is a real Aladdin's cave. A Crafts Council section sells contemporary works by British artists – one-off presents and future collectables – while the main, attractively laid-out section is filled with clever reproductions of 18th-century ceramics, antique dolls and teddy bears, a vast selection of William Morris memorabilia and lavish coffee-table art books. At the Science Museum, adults will find an unusual range of gadgetry and scientific instruments.

KING'S ROAD

The young and young at heart flock to this Chelsea thoroughfare for its boutiques and other interesting stores. A promenade can start at Sloane Square (Tube: Sloane Square) and take in the entire length of the long road, or just a fraction; either way there is a crop of coffee shops, from the chains such as Costa Coffee, Coffee Republic and

Starbucks to independent cafés, at which to fuel your progress.

Peter Jones department store (Sloane Square, SW1, tel: 020 7730 3434) is in Sloane Square itself. Whistles, Kookai, Warehouse, Oasis and Next begin a roll-call of mid-price fashion names as you begin to wander down the King's Road. Farther along, the vintage clothes store **Steinberg & Tolkien** (193 King's Road, SW3, tel: 020 7376 3660) has a dazzling array of garments from past decades, including original Pucci shirts, 1970s kaftans and cases of old jewelry and wacky accessories.

Renaissance (194 King's Road, SW3, tel: 020 7351 1557) is a divine store full of atmospheric candles to go with any decor. Choose from a range of floating, votive or aromatherapy candles. Downwind of the outlet **Lush** (123 King's Road, SW3, tel: 020 7376 8348), you can smell in advance the fragrant natural cosmetics before you see them: soaps sliced from huge blocks

to order, fizzing bath bombs and gooey hand-mixed face packs, plus fun packaging and labeling.

A branch of **Heal's** (234 King's Road, SW3, tel: 020 7349 8411) has nice things for the home, from furniture to photo frames, as does the fashionable **Designers' Guild** (267–271 & 275–277 King's Road, SW3, tel: 020 7351 5775) toward the World's End of the King's Road (Tube: West Brompton or Earls Court). Food fans might enjoy trekking this far along to discover the **Bluebird** Gastrodome (▶ 132) with its café, bar, restaurant and food and flower market. Check out the bakery's lovely fresh breads such as rosemary or spinach, the delicatessen counters and curious dry goods. Opposite, the sweet-toothed can indulge at **Rococo** chocolates (321 King's Road, SW3, tel: 020 7352 5857) with its artisan bars of dark and milk chocolate flavored with ingredients like Earl Grey tea, chili pepper, nutmeg, cardamom and wild mint leaves.

Where to...
Be Entertained

This is a cosmopolitan, well-heeled part of the city, with plenty of entertainment choices. Although it's an expensive area, there is no dearth of great-value venues.

MOVIE THEATERS

Choice is divided between the **two multi-screen UGC theaters**, showing recent releases (279 King's Road, SW3, tel: 0870 907 0710 and 142 Fulham Road, SW10, tel: 0870 907 0711. Tube: Earl's Court). **The Chelsea Cinema** (206 King's Road, SW3, tel: 020 7351 3742. Tube: Earl's Court) shows similar movies, with the bonus of the most comfortable movie theater seats in town. It also has a small bar. At the **Gate Cinema** (Notting Hill Gate, W11,

tel: 020 7727 4043. Tube: Notting Hill Gate) both trendy art-house movies and mainstream blockbusters are screened.

CLASSICAL MUSIC

The **Proms**, as the Henry Wood Promenade Concerts are more popularly known, are advertised by the BBC as the world's greatest music festival. Concerts are held nightly at the **Royal Albert Hall** (Kensington Gore, tel: 020 7589 8212. Tube: South Kensington) for a seven-week period every summer. Visiting international orchestras, soloists and conductors join the BBC Symphony Orchestra to perform a wide-ranging selection of music. If you are prepared to stand in line, you can buy inexpensive

tickets to "prom" or stand. Those with less stamina (but deeper pockets) can choose from a range of more expensive seats.

NIGHTLIFE

Nightclubs are not found in abundance in this part of the city. Try **Cuba** (11 Kensington High Street, W8, tel: 020 7938 4137. Tube: Kensington High Street), a chic place with a smart clientele. It offers a broad spectrum of Latin music, with occasional live bands.

If you like jazz, try the **606 Club** (90 Lots Road, SW10, tel: 020 7352 5953. Tube: Earl's Court), where groups such as the bluesy modern jazz Julian Siegel Quartet play. It is open to non-members. At the sophisticated **Pizza on the Park** (11–13 Knightsbridge, SW1, tel: 020 7235 5273. Tube: Hyde Park Corner), you can listen to live music. Jazz greats such as veteran singer George Melly have performed in the basement room.

THEATER

Whether shocking, disturbing or just plain brilliant, the **Royal Court** (Sloane Square, SW1, tel: 020 7565 5000. Tube: Sloane Square), home of the English Stage Company, has nurtured some of Britain's best modern playwrights, and is the place to see modern theater at its very best. A multi-million pound refurbishment has uplifted the experience for theatergoers, replacing cramped conditions in the two theaters with state-of-the-art facilities.

The **Holland Park Theatre** (Holland Park W8, tel: 020 7602 7856. Tube: Holland Park) is a popular open-air theater that operates only in the summer months. With the ruins of the 17th-century Holland House as a backdrop, and occasional accompaniment from the peacocks wandering freely through the park, the theater plays host to the Royal Ballet as well as offering a well-regarded opera season.

Covent Garden, Bloomsbury and Soho

PPLE MARKET

ART & CRAFT

Getting Your Bearings

Exploration of these districts underlines London's amazing variety: Within the space of a few streets an area's character can change from upscale to run down, from retail to residential, and from busy and exciting to genteel and refined.

★ Don't Miss

At Your Leisure

Covent Garden has gone through more changes than most London districts. Up until the 1970s it was the site of London's wholesale fruit and vegetable market, but when this moved south of the Thames, the market building was transformed into a small shopping center and craft market. Gentrification has since spread, and the market and surrounding area have become a vibrant shopping and entertainment district full of stores, market stands, fun museums, bars, cafés and restaurants.

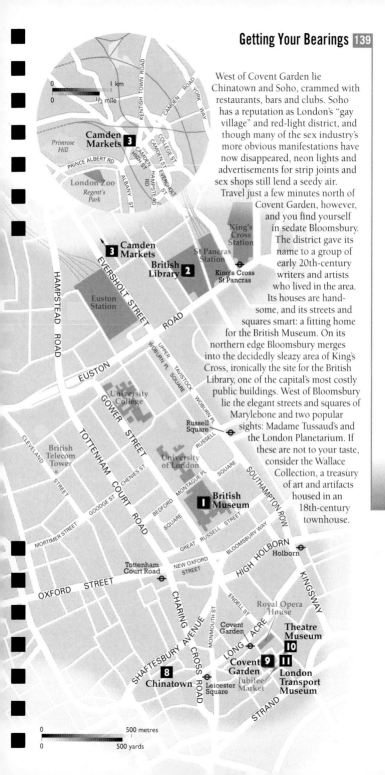

West of Covent Garden lie Chinatown and Soho, crammed with restaurants, bars and clubs. Soho has a reputation as London's "gay village" and red-light district, and though many of the sex industry's more obvious manifestations have now disappeared, neon lights and advertisements for strip joints and sex shops still lend a seedy air.

Travel just a few minutes north of Covent Garden, however, and you find yourself in sedate Bloomsbury. The district gave its name to a group of early 20th-century writers and artists who lived in the area. Its houses are handsome, and its streets and squares smart: a fitting home for the British Museum. On its northern edge Bloomsbury merges into the decidedly sleazy area of King's Cross, ironically the site for the British Library, one of the capital's most costly public buildings. West of Bloomsbury lie the elegant streets and squares of Marylebone and two popular sights: Madame Tussaud's and the London Planetarium. If these are not to your taste, consider the Wallace Collection, a treasury of art and artifacts housed in an 18th-century townhouse.

A variety of tempting cultural experiences awaits in a day that takes in the ancient treasures of the British Museum, the priceless books and manuscripts of the British Library, and the waxwork models of the rich, famous and notorious in Madame Tussaud's.

Covent Garden, Bloomsbury and Soho in a Day

9:00 am

Arrive at the ❶ British Museum (► 142–145) for when the Great Court opens at 9 am. Spend some time admiring this splendid new concourse, before exploring the museum itself, full of beautiful pieces from bygone civilizations (Elgin Marbles, left).

12:00 noon

Take lunch in one of the many cafés and pubs near the museum or bring along a picnic to eat in leafy Russell Square.

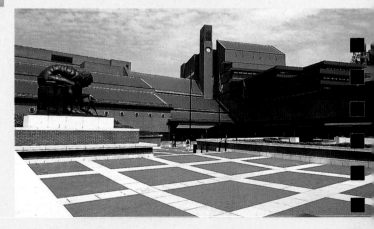

1:00 pm

From Russell Square catch a No. 91 bus or take a 30-minute walk through Bloomsbury to the **2** **British Library** (➤ 146–147). Look at the outside of the building from the spacious piazza (below left) then admire some of the world's loveliest old books and manuscripts. Stop for a coffee in the café here.

2:30 pm

The No. 30 bus takes you along Euston Road to Marylebone Road and **5** **Madame Tussaud's** (➤ 148–149). The wax-works are popular year-round and lines to get in are long, so try to buy your ticket in advance.

4:30 pm

Take the Underground from Baker Street to **9** **Covent Garden** (above, ➤ 150–151). The market, stores, street entertainers and the area's great choice of restaurants, pubs and bars make this a lively place to spend the early evening. It's a short walk from here to many West End theaters (➤ 160).

❶ British Museum

The British Museum houses one of the world's foremost collections, containing a wealth of antiquities illuminating the history of civilizations and cultures from across the globe. Founded in 1753 around the private collection of Sir Hans Sloane, it now possesses over 6 million artifacts arranged in a magnificent building with several miles of galleries. The exhibits on display include ancient sculpture, sublime paintings, exquisite jewelry and a host of other treasures.

The colonnaded main building of the British Museum was built in 1844 to replace the earlier Montagu House, which had become too small to house the museum's growing collection

The British Museum is vast, with more than enough beautiful exhibits to sustain several lengthy visits, so for those with only a short amount of time, the key to surviving and enjoying the museum is not to try to see it all in one visit. Be ruthlessly selective and try not to get too distracted *en route*.

Start by visiting the **(Queen Elizabeth II) Great Court.** This spectacular new concourse area, created by glassing over the museum's central courtyard, is part of an ongoing program of redevelopment. At its heart lies the beautiful 19th-century Reading Room, which

➕ 197 F3 ✉ Great Russell Street, WC1 ☎ 020 7323 8000; www.thebritish-museum.ac.uk 🕐 Main galleries: daily 10–5:30, Thu–Fri some galleries open late until 8:30. Great Court: Mon–Wed 9–9, Thu–Sat 9 am–11 pm, Sun 9–6; closed Jan 1, Good Fri, Dec 24-6 🍴 Cafés and restaurants
🚇 Holborn, Tottenham Court Road, Russell Square 🚌 Tottenham Court Road, northbound, and Gower Street, southbound 10, 24, 29, 73, 134; Southampton Row 68, 91; New Oxford Street 19, 25, 38, 55, 98; Great Russell Street 7
♿ Free

Right: The Egyptian Sculpture Gallery is home to statues, sarcophagi and the Rosetta Stone, one of the most important artifacts in the British Museum

Below: The Great Court, the largest covered square in Europe

until recently housed the British Library (► 146–147) but is now open to the general public. Marx, Lenin, George Bernard Shaw and hundreds of other luminaries studied here. The Great Court serves as the museum's central information area: Pick up a museum plan before starting your exploration of the galleries.

The **Eygptian galleries,** which house one of the best collections of Egyptian antiquities outside Egypt, are among the museum's highlights. Funerary art and artifacts dominate, with exquisitely decorated coffins, mummies, sarcophagi, jewelry, models and scrolls. The gilded inner coffin of Henutmehyt (around 1290 BC) is particularly impressive. Also look out for the case containing "Ginger," the 5,000-year-old mummified body of an Egyptian man, whose leathery remains always draw a crowd. He still has a few tufts of red hair, but is missing his left index finger (it was "collected" by an early visitor to the museum).

The most important exhibit in these galleries, and perhaps the entire museum, is the **Rosetta Stone** (196 BC). Its significance lies in the three languages of its inscriptions: Greek at the bottom, Egyptian hieroglyphs at the top, a cursive form of the Egyptian between the two. Discovered accidentally in 1799, the stone enabled Egyptian hieroglyphs to be deciphered for the first time, allowing much of Egyptian civilization to be understood. Less important, but more more visually arresting, is the

Suggested Route
Follow this route to cover some of the museum's highlights with minimum fuss.

First floor:
Room 4 Egyptian Sculpture Gallery
Rooms 6–10 Assyrian Galleries
Room 18 The Sculptures of the
   Parthenon

Second floor:
Room 41 Early Medieval (Sutton Hoo)
Room 49 Weston Gallery of Roman
   Britain (Mildenhall Treasure)
Rooms 62–66 Egyptian Galleries

huge granite **head of Rameses II**, which towers over
the gallery: It was carved for the ruler's memorial temple in
Thebes in the 13th century BC.

The museum's most controversial sculptures are the **Elgin
Marbles**, named after Lord Elgin, a British diplomat who
brought them to England in 1816. Most are taken from a
5th-century BC frieze removed from the Parthenon, the most
important temple in ancient Athens, and probably depict a festival in honor of Athena, the city's patron goddess. Modern
Greece believes the Marbles should be returned, claiming it is
wrong that a foreign museum should possess such important
national cultural relics.

The Assyrians, who lived in what is now northern Iraq, are
represented in the museum by, among other things, the entrance
of **Khorsabad, Palace of Sargon** (721–705 BC), a glorious
example of the massive carvings of winged bulls with human
heads that guarded their palaces. Equally beguiling are the
reliefs of King Ashurbanipal, the last great Assyrian king; they
depict a lion hunt, and once adorned his palace in Ninevah.

British artifacts are also celebrated. The 7th-century Anglo-
Saxon **Sutton Hoo Ship Burial exhibits** – weapons and

An imposing
reconstruction
of the Nereid
monument from
Xanthos in the
southwest of
present-day
Turkey

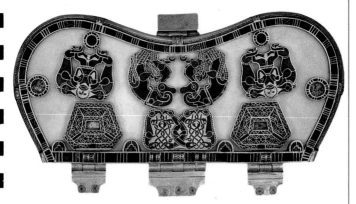

Above: A purse lid, one of the Sutton Hoo Ship Burial exhibits, displays fine Anglo-Saxon craftmanship

helmets in particular – provide a valuable insight into the Dark Ages, a period of British and European history about which relatively little is known. The treasures were found in 1939 during excavations of ancient burial mounds close to the River Deben near the town of Woodbridge in Suffolk, a site which, before the construction of sea walls, lay just 607 feet from the high-water level. The **Mildenhall Treasure**, an important collection of 4th-century Roman silverware, was found at Mildenhall, in Suffolk, just a few years later. Some mystery still surrounds the discovery of the treasure, which was not immediately declared to the authorities. Its centerpiece is the 18-pound Great Dish, decorated with images of Neptune, the sea god, with a beard of seaweed and dolphins leaping from his hair.

TAKING A BREAK
The **Coffee Gallery** (23 Museum Street, WC1, tel: 020 7436 0455), serving salads, filled bagels, chili chicken and mixed *meze*, is a great place to stop for a light lunch.

BRITISH MUSEUM: INSIDE INFO

Top tips The museum has two entrances: The main one on Great Russell Street and a quieter one on **Montague Place**.
• Video and still photography (excluding flash) is generally allowed.
• **Guided tours** of the museum's highlights (60 and 90 mins.; charge) or individual galleries (50 mins.; free) are available. For further information, or to book, ask at information points in the Great Court. Audio-guides are also available.

In more detail The **Mexican Gallery (Room 27)** contains several impressive displays, the loveliest of which are the turquoise mosaic statues from the Mixtec–Aztec era (1400–1521).
• If you have time, admire the craftsmanship of the gold and silver **Oxus Treasure (Room 51)**, a collection of Persian artifacts dating from the 5th or 4th century BC.

One to miss The famous **Portland Vase**, a piece of Roman blown glass, is actually rather small and unimpressive. Repairs carried out after it was smashed into a couple of hundred pieces by a drunken visitor in 1845 are all too clearly visible.

2 British Library

The British Library ranks alongside the National Library of Congress in Washington and the Bibliothèque Nationale in Paris as one of the three greatest libraries in the world. Its contents include some of the world's most incredible printed treasures. Exhibits span almost three millennia, from the Buddhist *Diamond Sutra* of AD 868, the world's oldest printed book, up to the modern manuscripts of Paul McCartney and John Lennon. Along the way they take in Shakespeare's First

Folio, the Gutenberg Bible, the Magna Carta and the notebooks of Leonardo da Vinci.

The purpose-built, modern library buildings, grouped around an attractive central plaza, provide an airy, attractive, user-friendly space in which to enjoy the collection.

The **John Ritblat Gallery** contains some of the library's principal treasures, including maps, sacred religious texts, historical documents, letters and literary and musical manuscripts. The gallery is remarkable for the fame, age,

The binding of the Lindisfarne Gospels (about AD 698)

breadth and quality of its collection. The light is kept low to protect the material and the atmosphere is almost hallowed – as indeed it should be in the presence of the Lindisfarne Gospels and Bedford Hours, two of the loveliest early English illuminated manuscripts. Among the other treasures on display are original manuscripts by Jane Austen and Charlotte Brontë, scores by Mozart and Handel, including that of the *Messiah*, letters from Gandhi, and Lord Nelson's last (unfinished) love letter to Lady Hamilton.

For an interactive experience head for **Turning the Pages**, a unique computer-based system (just off the John Ritblat Gallery) that allows visitors to "browse" through some of the treasures a page at a time.

🚩 197 F5   ✉ 96 Euston Road, NW1   ☎ 020 7412 7332
🕐 Mon–Fri 9:30–6 (also Tue 6–8), Sat 9:30–5, Sun and public holidays 11–5
🍴 Restaurant, coffee shop and café   🚇 King's Cross
🚌 10, 30, 73, 91, 99   💷 Free

The library's two other galleries offer a more practical look at books. The **Pearson Gallery** interprets and enlivens the library's great collections and is the location for special exhibitions. There is even a small reading area to sit and enjoy a selection of books. The **Workshop of Words, Sounds and Images** investigates the technology of book production, printing and sound recording. It offers an interactive, computer-based chance to design a book page – there are often also printing demonstrations.

TAKING A BREAK

Visit the library's café or restaurant (▶ Inside Info, below). Alternatively, try **Patisserie Deux Amis** (63 Judd Street, WC1, tel: 020 7383 7029), a simple café serving filled baguettes and delicious cakes.

Edouard Paolozzi's statue of Newton (1995) in the British Library's piazza depicts him measuring the universe with a pair of dividers

VITAL STATISTICS

❏ The library basement is equivalent to over five stories and holds 500 miles of shelving.

❏ Some 12 million books are stored in the basement, but the library's total collection numbers over 150 million items.

❏ The library receives a free copy of every book, comic, newspaper, map and magazine published in the United Kingdom. This means it receives an average of 10,000 new items weekly.

❏ The library building was mooted in the 1950s but opened only in 1998, by which time it had cost three times its original budget.

BRITISH LIBRARY: INSIDE INFO

Top tips Visit the **café or restaurant**, as you can enjoy some of the best views of the central glass tower that houses the 65,000 leather-bound volumes of King George III's library from here.

In more detail Guided tours provide an excellent introduction to the history and workings of the library (1 hour, additional charge, Monday, Wednesday and Friday, Saturday 10:30 am and 3 pm. Tours on Tuesday 6:30 pm and Sunday 11:30 am and 3 pm include include a visit to one of the reading rooms.

5 Madame Tussaud's

One of London's most popular tourist attractions, Madame Tussaud's offers you the chance to meet James Bond, see how tall actor Arnold Schwarzenegger really is and have your photograph taken with boxing legend Mohammad Ali – or at least waxwork models of these and over 400 other famous people. A visit provides a fun-packed couple of hours' entertainment for adults and children alike.

A splitting image – actress and singer Kylie Minogue, with her waxwork twin

The displays proper start with **The Garden Party**, where many of the collection's contemporary figures – including film stars and sporting greats – are portrayed as if relaxing at a social gathering. You move on to displays detailing the story of Madame Tussaud, who learned her art in 18th-century France, came to Britain with a traveling show and, 33 years later, in 1835, founded the museum. A sequence of exhibits shows how the models are made. Each model takes about six months and costs over $50,000 to create. Look out for the shelves of old body parts, including heads, of ex-celebrities who have faded from the

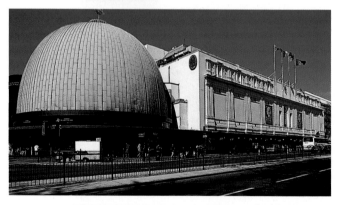

🞢 196 B4 ✉ Marylebone Road, NW1
☎ 0870 400 3000;
www.madame-tussauds.com
🕐 Mon–Fri 10–5:30 (last entry), Sat–Sun 9:30–5:30; closed Dec 25

🍴 Café Tussaud's for snacks, but a better choice in Baker Street nearby
🚇 Baker Street
🚌 13, 18, 27, 30, 74, 82, 113, 139, 159, 274
💷 Expensive

FACTS AND FIGURES

❏ Early techniques involved casts being made of the model's head. Napoleon had to have straws stuck up his nostrils so that he could breathe as his cast was made, and was so distressed he held Josephine's hand throughout.

❏ All the hair used on the models is real and is regularly washed and styled.

❏ The wax used is similar to candle wax and the exhibition has no windows so that models don't melt in the sunlight.

limelight and lost their place in the show.

Upstairs in the **Grand Hall** there are models of religious leaders, members of the Royal Family, politicians and world leaders as well as figures from the arts including Picasso, Beethoven and The Beatles.

From here you plunge into the **Chamber of Horrors**, perhaps the exhibition's best-known – and certainly most ghoulish – section. Torture, execution and murder are dealt with, together with lots of gruesome sound effects. It's a part of the show those with young children may wish to avoid.

The climax of the exhibition is the **Spirit of London** section, in which visitors take a ride in a model taxi through a fabulously colorful tableau of 400 years of London's history.

As if it were yesterday – John, Paul, George and Ringo, as they appeared at the start of their career

TAKING A BREAK

Try the dim sum at the hugely popular **Royal China** (40 Baker Street, W1, tel: 020 7487 4688).

MADAME TUSSAUD'S: INSIDE INFO

Top tips The exhibition is hugely popular and lines to get in are often long. To avoid the lines, **buy tickets in advance by credit card**, which allows you to enter by the ticket holders' entrance. There is a small extra fee for tickets bought in this way.

• The exhibition space opens a half-hour earlier in **school holidays** (phone for details), but avoid visiting at this time, if possible. The exhibition is quieter later in the afternoon: if you arrive by 4:30 you'll still have time to see everything.

• A **combined ticket** for Madame Tussaud's and the adjoining London Planetarium (▶ 153) will save you money if you intend seeing both.

9 Covent Garden

When London's wholesale fruit and vegetable market moved out of Covent Garden in the 1970s the scene was set for its

transformation into one of the city's most lively, entertaining and popular districts. Weekends are best for exploring the superb shopping, market and entertainment area, with plenty of excellent bars, cafés and restaurants. There are some superb museums, top London theaters and the world-renowned Royal Opera House.

The district's heart is the Piazza, the square surrounding the restored 19th-century market building that now houses small shops and the crafts stands of the Apple Market. Close by is the revamped Royal Opera House and the indoor Jubilee Market (clothes, crafts and leather goods), while the Theatre Museum (► 155) and the London Transport Museum (► 155) will provide a good couple of hours' diversion.

Street performers entertain Covent Garden visitors

Right: Fruit and vegetable stalls in Covent Garden have given way to a wide variety of cafés, bars and craft stalls

One of the piazza's highlights is the variety of street entertainers who congregate here, embracing everything from Chinese orchestras and South American pan pipe musicians to acrobats, mime artists and didgeridoo players. They generate much of the "buzz" and atmosphere of the place. The many small streets, especially Neal Street and the area north of the Covent Garden Underground station, are also well worth exploring for their individual and unusual stores (► 159) and tucked-away cafés, bars and restaurants.

✚ 200 A3 🚇 Covent Garden 🚌 Along Strand 6, 9, 11, 13, 15, 23, 77A, 91, 176

COVENT GARDEN: INSIDE INFO

Top tips Don't leave Covent Garden without wandering down **Neal Street**. Interesting stores here include **Neal Street East** (5 Neal Street, WC2, tel: 020 7240 0135), which specializes in Asian goods, and **The Tea House** (15 Neal Street, WC2, tel: 020 7240 7539), selling a huge range of teas and tea pots.

• Don't miss **Neal's Yard Remedies** (15 Neal's Yard, WC2, tel: 020 7379 7222), where you can buy herbal remedies, top-quality oils and toiletries. The store also has a good selection of books on herbal and alternative medicine.

• For delicious English cheeses, try **Neal's Yard Dairy** (17 Shorts Gardens, WC2, tel: 020 7240 5700). Or stop at **Monmouth Coffee Company** (➤ 157), for one of the best cups of coffee in London.

Hidden gems Children and adults alike will love the **Cabaret Mechanical Theatre**, an exhibition of wonderfully witty, old-fashioned hands-on automatons down in the lower part of the central market building.

At Your Leisure

3 Camden Markets

The conglomeration of several markets, spreading out from Camden Lock along Chalk Farm Road and Camden High Street, draws many visitors to Camden Town. Sunday, when all the markets are open, is the best day to visit, though individual markets are open on other days. Be warned; the whole area is usually extremely crowded, especially in the summer. The market is particularly good for modern clothing, jewelry and crafts.

🚹 Off map 197 E5

Camden Lock

Renovated warehouses beside the canal are packed solid with stands selling arts, crafts, old and new clothing, tapes and CDs, plus food and drink.

🕐 Daily 10–6

Camden Canal Market

This market is located to the north of the canal between Chalk Farm Road

and Castle Haven Road. The entrance is small, but the place is packed with stands selling collectable items such as books and clothes – even bicycles.

🕐 Fri–Sun 10–6

Stables Market

This is the most northerly of the markets (off Chalk Farm Road). It sells pretty much the same range of items as Camden Lock but with some furniture and antiques as well.

🕐 Sat–Sun 9–5; Mon–Fri 9–5, reduced number of stands

Electric Market

Selling secondhand clothes, plus some new items, this market has an emphasis on the weird and way out.

✉ Camden High Street, just north of Camden Town Underground
🕐 Sun 9–5:30

Camden Market

Look here for old and new clothing, jewelry and audio tapes.

✉ Camden High Street 🕐 Thu–Sun 9–5:30

4 Regent's Park

Regent's Park ranks alongside St. James's Park as one of central London's loveliest green spaces (► 14). Fringed by the glorious Regency architecture of John Nash, it is loved by locals and visitors alike for its rose garden, its open-air theater, boating lake and **London Zoo**. The zoo, founded in 1826, was once *the* place to be seen. Though now much less fashionable, it is still popular with families. Entertaining shows and talks reinforce the zoo's conservation remit.

An oft-overlooked park attraction is a trip on the Regent's Canal. Built in 1820, it runs for 8 miles between chic Little Venice in west London to Limehouse in the Docklands, where it

Regent's Canal, a peaceful backwater

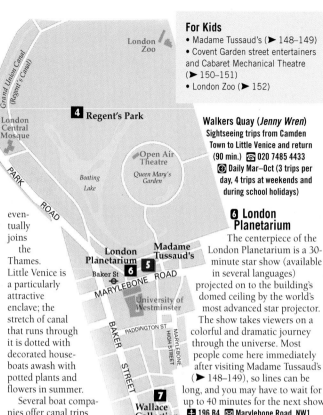

For Kids
- Madame Tussaud's (▶ 148–149)
- Covent Garden street entertainers and Cabaret Mechanical Theatre (▶ 150–151)
- London Zoo (▶ 152)

Walkers Quay (*Jenny Wren*)
Sightseeing trips from Camden Town to Little Venice and return (90 min.) ☎ 020 7485 4433
🕑 Daily Mar–Oct (3 trips per day, 4 trips at weekends and during school holidays)

eventually joins the Thames. Little Venice is a particularly attractive enclave; the stretch of canal that runs through it is dotted with decorated houseboats awash with potted plants and flowers in summer.

Several boat companies offer canal trips between Little Venice and Camden Lock. Or, a gentle stroll along the canal banks is a delightful antidote to the sights and sounds of the city.

✚ 196 B5

London Zoo
✉ Regent's Park ☎ 020 7722 3333
🕑 Daily 10–5:30, Apr–Oct, 10–4 Nov–Mar 💷 Expensive

London Waterbus Company
☎ 020 7482 2660 🕑 Sat–Sun 10–5 all year; Mon–Fri 10–5 end Mar–Oct. Hourly departures.

Jason's Trip
☎ 020 7286 3428 🕑 Three times daily late Mar–Oct

6 London Planetarium
The centerpiece of the London Planetarium is a 30-minute star show (available in several languages) projected on to the building's domed ceiling by the world's most advanced star projector. The show takes viewers on a colorful and dramatic journey through the universe. Most people come here immediately after visiting Madame Tussaud's (▶ 148–149), so lines can be long, and you may have to wait for up to 40 minutes for the next show.

✚ 196 B4 ✉ Marylebone Road, NW1 ☎ 0870 400 3000 🕑 Daily 10–5:30, last show 5. Not recommended for young children; closed Dec 25 🍴 Good choice in Baker Street nearby 🚇 Baker Street 🚌 18, 27, 30 💷 Moderate. Combined tickets available with Madame Tussaud's (▶ 148)

7 Wallace Collection
This remarkable collection of *objets d'art* is made all the more alluring by its setting, Manchester House, a beautiful 18th-century mansion acquired in 1797 by the 2nd Marquess of Hertford. Its collection of artifacts was bequeathed to the nation on condition it should never be sold, loaned or removed from central London.

Every room is filled with treasures, though most people's favorite is Room 22, where a wonderful collection of

works by Titian, Rubens, Murillo, Van Dyck and others is on display. The collection's best-known work, Frans Hals's *The Laughing Cavalier*, is also here. The portrait of an unknown young man was painted in 1624. While obviously a figure of substance, the man in question is neither laughing nor a cavalier: The title was coined in 1888 when the picture was lent to the Royal Academy Old Masters Exhibition. Nearby is another portrait of an unknown sitter, Velázquez's *Lady With A Fan*.

Manchester House provides an elegant backdrop to the Wallace Collection

The collection's sheer variety is its principal charm. The breadth of exhibits provides the opportunity to admire things you might normally overlook, be it Sèvres porcelain, fine pieces of furniture, detailed miniatures or 18th-century paintings. The displays of armor are some of the best in the country outside the Tower of London.

➕ 196 B3 ✉ Hertford House, Manchester Square, W1 ☎ 020 7935 0687; www.wallace-collection.com
🕐 Mon–Sat 10–5, Sun 2–5
🍴 Courtyard restaurant 🚇 Bond Street
🚌 2, 10, 12, 13, 30, 74, 82, 94, 113, 137, 274 🎟 Free

Left: Gerrard Street, at the heart of
London's Chinatown, is crammed with
restaurants

8 Chinatown

The few blocks around Gerrard Street
provide a magnet for London's
60,000-strong Chinese community.
Many live elsewhere, but flock here
on Sundays when the area is most
lively. The streets are full of Chinese
signs, restaurants (► 156), grocers
and bookstores. Even the telephone
boxes resemble pagodas.

➕ 197 F2 ✉ Around Gerrard
Street, W1 🚇 Leicester Square 🚌 14,
19, 24, 29, 38, 176

9 Theatre Museum

The museum has a wide range of
artifacts from some 400 years of
British theater history
and is unmissable for
anyone who enjoys the
performing arts.
Younger visitors should
enjoy the museum's
program of activities,
especially the costume
workshops and stage
make-up demonstra-
tions. Most of the
museum guides are
"resting" actors, and use
their professional skills
to entertain their
audience.

The museum's
displays embrace every
aspect of theater: Gilbert
and Sullivan and the
Music Hall, for example, have
their own sections, and
many theatrical characters
are featured, including Sir
Henry Irving, Ellen Terry and
Nöel Coward. Other sections
look at the technical aspects of
the theater, notably "The Wind in
the Willows – From Page to
Stage," which details the
process of creating a production from finance to
casting, design, marketing,
the stage manager's role and the
voice coaching given to actors.

➕ 200 B4 ✉ Russell Street, Covent
Garden, WC2 ☎ 020 7943 4700;
www.theatremuseum.org 🕐 Tue–Sun
10–6 (last admission 5:30) 🚇 Covent
Garden 🚌 Along Strand 6, 9, 11, 13, 15,
23, 77A, 91, 176 🖐 Free

11 London Transport Museum

This museum gives the history of
London over the last 200 years
through its buses, trams and trains. It
looks at the way in which transportation has affected and still affects the
lives of people in the city, and shows
what it takes to move millions of
travelers around the capital daily.
Visitors can see how the Underground
and bus systems were built and operate today and can drive an Underground train simulator. The museum
looks forward as well as back, covering current transporta-
tion issues, such as the
impact of increasing car
ownership on the
capital's roads.

➕ 200 B3 ✉ Covent
Garden, WC2 ☎ 020 7565
7299; www.ltmuseum.co.uk
🕐 Sat–Thu 10–6,
Fri 11–6. Last admission
5:15pm 🍴 Café
🚇 Covent Garden
🚌 Along Strand 6, 9, 11,
13, 15, 23, 77A, 91, 176
🖐 Moderate

Dramatic props at the
Theatre Museum

Where to...
Eat and Drink

Prices
Expect to pay per person for a meal excluding drinks and service

$ under £25 $$ £25–£50 $$$ over £50

Alastair Little Soho $$
Everything about Alastair Little's eponymous restaurant is understated – from the bare aquamarine walls and stripped floorboards, to the casual, but informed service and the fresh, deceptively simple food. An Italian influence sits well with the refreshingly seasonal ingredients, the quality of which shines through in every dish. The fixed-price menus (there is no à la carte) are very good value for money.

🕂 197 E2 ⊠ 49 Frith Street, W1 ☎ 020 7734 5183 🕒 Lunch: Mon–Fri noon–3. Dinner: Mon–Sat 6–11 🚇 Leicester Square

Bank $$
An enormous contemporary brasserie, this is undoubtedly the most colorful of London's large-scale restaurants, where there's something for everyone at any time of the day. The menu combines French favorites with new metropolitan ideas. All dishes are highly enjoyable and of a consistently good standard. The waiting staff provides fast, super-efficient and polished service.

🕂 200 B4 ⊠ 1 Kingsway, WC2 ☎ 020 7379 9797; fax: 020 7379 9014 🕒 Mon–Sat noon–2.45, 5.30–11, Sun 11.30–3, 5.30–9.30 🚇 Holborn

Christopher's $–$$
Set on two floors in a grand Victorian building, this lively restaurant serves some of the best classic American food in London. The steaks, specially imported from the United States, Maine lobsters, tasty broiled meats and Maryland crab cakes are unmissable; portions are ample. Christopher's is popular: Reservations are recommended. The café-bar has greater informality and a menu of salads and sandwiches.

🕂 200 B3 ⊠ 18 Wellington Street, WC2 ☎ 020 7240 4222; fax: 020 7836 3506 🕒 Lunch: Mon–Fri noon–2.45, Sat–Sun 11.30–4 (brunch). Dinner: Mon–Sat 5–12.45 am 🚇 Covent Garden

Fung Shing $$
Chinatown may be wall-to-wall with Chinese restaurants, and Lisle Street in particular a crowded, run-down part of it, but the long-standing Fung Shing remains one of the best places to eat. The high quality, authentic Cantonese food which it serves further distinguishes it from its neighbors. The staff is adept and patient at explaining the menu.

🕂 197 F1 ⊠ 15 Lisle Street, WC2 ☎ 020 7437 1539; fax: 020 7734 0284 🕒 Daily noon–11.30 🚇 Leicester Square

Ibla $$
The decor may be rather garishly colored, with glossy puce paneling in one room and shiny fuchsia in the other reflecting the blinding light of the chandeliers; but this is the only nod to decoration. The sparse interior is in contrast to the exoticism of the menu, which is set at three or four courses. Though described in Italian, there's a strong French accent in the style, which is marked by imagination and talent. This is shown in combinations that take in pig's trotter with prawns and snails in a mustard balsamic sauce.

🕂 196 B4 ⊠ 89 Marylebone High Street, W1M ☎ 0207 224 3799 🕒 Noon–2.30, 7–10.15 🚇 Regent's Park

The Ivy $$

The Ivy ranks as one of London's most fashionable eating places, close to achieving cult status; regulars return again and again for their favorite dishes. What they enjoy is best described as classic brasserie food. Traditional British ideas are tempered by modern European and oriental additions. Over a dozen wines are available by the glass. Reserving well in advance is an absolute essential.

➕ 197 F2 ⌧ 1 West Street, Covent Garden, WC2 ☎ 020 7836 4751; fax: 020 7240 9333 ⌚ Daily noon–3 (also Sun 3–3:30), 5:30–midnight ⛔ Leicester Square, Covent Garden

J. Sheekey $$

A major facelift injected new life into this restaurant, one of the oldest and best known seafood restaurants in the capital. Run by the team responsible for such gastronomic temples as The Ivy and Le Caprice, J. Sheekey's is the place to go for traditional British fish dishes.

A selection of modern creations add an extra dimension to the menu.

➕ 197 F1 ⌧ 28–32 St. Martin's Court, WC2 ☎ 020 7240 2565 ⌚ Daily noon–3 (also Sun 3–3:30), 5:30–midnight ⛔ Leicester Square

Lindsay House $$

Some strong reminders that this was once a private Georgian house remain, incuding having to ring the bell in order to be admitted. The restful cream color scheme, enhanced by some stylish modern touches, however, is sympathetic. Irish chef Richard Corrigan has won great accolades for his cooking. His Celtic roots are still very evident in his gutsy, almost robust style, but his creations also pronounce a delicate touch. Offal is something of a passion for Corrigan, and his fish dishes are particularly imaginative.

➕ 197 E2 ⌧ 21 Romilly Street, W1 ☎ 020 7439 0450; fax: 020 7437 7349 ⌚ Lunch: Mon–Fri 12:30–3. Dinner: Mon–Sat 6–10:45. Closed last 2 weeks Aug ⛔ Leicester Square

Mezzo $$

This is one of the largest eateries in Europe and high standards are consistent at Sir Terence Conran's Soho branch. The lively Mezzonine (on the first floor), specializes in Pacific Rim food in comfortable canteen-style surroundings. The flagship basement restaurant, Mezzo, continues that theme, but includes some modern European ideas. Shellfish from the excellent crustacea bar is recommended.

➕ 197 E2 ⌧ 100 Wardour Street, W1 ☎ 020 7314 4000 ⌚ Mezzo: lunch Wed–Sun noon–2:30. Dinner Mon–Thu 6–11:30, Fri–Sat 6–12:30, Sun 6–10:30. Mezzonine: lunch Mon–Sat noon–2:30; dinner Mon–Sat 5:30–11:30 (also Fri–Sat 11:30–12:30 am) ⛔ Piccadilly Circus

Monmouth Coffee Company $

This is one of Soho's best-kept secrets. From the front is nothing more than a store selling bags of coffee beans, but at the back are eight tables, newspapers to read and

a delectable selection of pastries. It's the perfect place to stop, relax and sample some great coffees from the wide-ranging stock.

➕ 197 F2 ⌧ 27 Monmouth Street, WC2 ☎ 020 7645 3560 ⛔ Mon–Sat 9–6, Sun 11–5 ⛔ Covent Garden

The Orrery $$

This is one of the smallest restaurants in the Conran group, with just 80 seats, plus a shop and food store. However, the family design traits are all there: arched windows, lots of natural lighting, blond wood; a classy, stylish look. The short menu explores French classics, giving them a modern twist. The food bears many of Conran's trademark Mediterranean characteristics; raw ingredients especially have a true freshness and are of the best quality.

➕ 196 B3 ⌧ 55–57 Marylebone High Street, W1 ☎ 020 7616 8000; fax: 020 7616 8080 ⌚ Lunch: daily noon–2:45. Dinner: Mon–Sat 7–10:45, Sun 7–10:15 ⛔ Baker Street, Regent's Park

Le Palais du Jardin $$

This vast, popular brasserie right at the heart of Covent Garden has a strong Parisian feel, especially with the all-day seafood counter at the front, and the hustle and bustle of traditionally clad waiters. It is the seafood – lobster in particular – that those in the know come here for, but there is also a varied selection of meat dishes. This is a great place for a pre-theater meal.

✚ 200 A4 ⊠ 136 Long Acre, WC2
☎ 020 7379 5353; fax: 020 7379 1846
⏰ Mon–Sat noon–3, 5:30–midnight (3–5:30 limited menu), Sun noon–11
Ⓜ Covent Garden, Leicester Square

Pâtisserie Valerie $

The cramped but cozy old-fashioned tearoom is a Soho institution with shared tables and motherly waitresses; you won't want to leave. The patisserie is superb (just check out the window display), but there are also good salads, Croque Monsieur and savory quiches to go with tea, coffee or hot chocolate.

✚ 197 E2 ⊠ 44 Old Compton Street, W1 ☎ 020 7437 3466 ⏰ Mon–Sat 8–8, Sun 9:30–7 Ⓜ Leicester Square

La Porte des Indes $$

This is a fabulous Indian restaurant, filled with lush, tropical greenery and decked out in rich colors. The kitchen explores the culinary relationship between France and its Indian colonies through such dishes as beignets d'aubergines – slices of eggplant filled with cheese and herb pate. Lunch consists of a spectacular buffet, which offers one of the best-value meal deals in the area.

✚ 196 A2 ⊠ 32 Bryanston Street, W1 ☎ 020 7224 0055; fax: 020 7224 1144 ⏰ Lunch: Mon–Fri noon–2:30, Sun noon–3:30. Dinner: Mon–Sat 6:30–10:30, Sun 7–11:30 Ⓜ Marble Arch

Quo Vadis $$–$$$

The restaurant is the epitome of London style, where the megatalents of chef Marco Pierre White and artist Damien Hirst merge. The contemporary restaurant is filled with Hirst's startling art (the flayed bovine heads preserved in formaldehyde are in the upstairs bar). The cooking is classic with a French twist. Larousse Gastronomique dictionary definitions pepper the menu: sauce diable, sauce Bercy, matched with more than a streak of modernism.

✚ 197 E2 ⊠ 26–29 Dean Street, W1 ☎ 020 7437 9585; fax: 020 7434 9972 ⏰ Lunch: Mon–Fri noon–3. Dinner: Mon–Sat 6–11:30, Sun 6–10:30 Ⓜ Leicester Square

Stephen Bull Restaurant $$

This is a small, intimate room, in which the tables are necessarily close and the only decoration a controlled use of color. The focus is firmly on the food. Short menus, a simple, light, touch and a straightforward approach show Stephen Bull maintaining the innovative streak that has kept him at the forefront of the London culinary scene for a generation. A good choice of wines are available by the half bottle and the glass. It is essential to make a reservation here.

✚ 196 B3 ⊠ 5–7 Blandford Street, W1 ☎ 020 7486 9696; fax: 020 7486 5067 ⏰ Lunch: Mon–Fri 12:15–2:30. Dinner: Mon–Sat 6:30–10:30 Ⓜ Bond Street

Vasco & Piero's Pavilion $–$$

Dining out in Soho tends to be an overwhelmingly trend-driven affair, so it's to be welcomed that this much-loved Soho institution is still going strong. The small space is nothing special: peach-colored walls hung with modern art, cramped tables and hard metal chairs. The daily changing menu is brief but offers plenty of choice in modern Italian dishes. Service is speedily efficient without rushing diners. Bargain hunters should investigate the three-course set-dinner menu.

✚ 197 D2/E2 ⊠ 15 Poland Street, W1 ☎ 020 7437 8774 ⏰ Noon–3, 6–11 (from 7 pm Sat). Closed lunch Sat, all Sun

Where to... Shop

This central part of London acts as a visitor-magnet and shopping here takes in both extremes of tourist clichés and sophisticated specialty goods.

COVENT GARDEN

Covent Garden's pedestrianized Piazza (Tube: Covent Garden) is a popular visitor's choice (▶ 150–151). Traders here are keen to capitalize on the crowds and many stores stay open till 7 or 8 pm.

The Market itself is a good starting point. Stand and watch street performers or meander the arcades. **The Candle Shop** (30 The Market, WC2, tel: 020 7836 9815) sells all styles, perfumes and colors of candle. **Culpeper Herbalists** (8 The Market, WC2, tel: 020 7379 6698) stocks English herbs, oils, bath salts, potpourri and toiletries that make great presents. **Benjamin Pollock's Toy Shop** (44 The Market, WC2, tel: 020 7379 7866) is an amazing emporium of hand-made puppets, puppet theaters and other toys.

If you're looking for clothes, British designer **Paul Smith** (43 Floral Street, WC2, tel: 020 7379 7133) sells superb casual wear, sharp suits, and unusual socks, ties and cufflinks. **Robot** (37 Floral Street, WC2, tel: 020 7836 6156) is stocked with trendy sunglasses, hats and cool clothing for men.

BLOOMSBURY

The **British Museum's store** (Great Russell Street, WC1, tel: 020 7323 8613, Tube: Holborn, Tottenham Court Road, Russell Square) sells reproduction jewelry, Egyptian artifacts and Michelangelo mementos.

Bloomsbury is also the traditional home of London's publishing houses, so there are **bookstores** galore. (Tube: Charing Cross Road (Tube: Leicester Square) is the place for bookworms: **Foyles, Books etc, Blackwell's** and **Waterstone's** are the big four. **Any Amount of Books** (62 Charing Cross Road, WC2, tel: 020 7240 8140. Tube: Tottenham Court Road) sells secondhand books and has a bargain basement. **Ulysses** (40 Museum Street, WC1, tel: 020 7831 1600. Tube: Tottenham Court Road) specializes in first editions.

SOHO

Chinatown lies at the heart of Soho, and Gerrard Street is at the heart of Chinatown. It is the cultural and financial center of Britain's Chinese community, with an amazing choice of restaurants and Chinese stores.

Soho is better known for its restaurants than for conventional shopping. Food, however, is a serious draw. **Berwick Street Market** (Berwick Street), a Monday to Saturday "fruit and veg" extravaganza, is worth a visit. On Old Compton Street there are **I. Camisa & Co.** (35 Old Compton Street, W1, tel: 020 7437 7610. Tube: Leicester Square), which sells Italian deli foods, the **Algerian Coffee Store** (52 Old Compton Street, W1, tel: 020 7437 2480. Tube: Leicester Square) for a range of fresh coffees, and the wonderful **Pâtisserie Valerie** for delicious French cakes (▶ 158).

American Retro (35 Old Compton Street, W1, tel: 020 7734 3477. Tube: Leicester Square) is a great source funky accessories. In Brewer Street check out the **Vintage Magazine Shop** (39–43 Brewer Street, W1, tel: 020 7439 8525. Tube: Piccadilly Circus), a good place to search out an old movie poster or rare movie and music magazines.

London's clubbers help to keep places open later in Soho than in other parts of the capital.

Where to...
Be Entertained

This part of London is crammed with theaters, clubs, movie theaters and bars, and on a Saturday night it can seem as if the whole metropolis has squeezed itself into taxis or traveled on the Tube to surface at Leicester Square and Covent Garden. Late on a Friday or Saturday night the pavements are still thronged with people and the atmosphere is lively. There is much to take in when considering the choice of entertainment.

THEATER

The choice ranges from the long-running blockbusters of Shaftesbury Avenue to Off-West End at the

Donmar Warehouse (tel: 020 7369 1732. Tube: Covent Garden). Although you can go directly to the individual theater's box office, you might be able to pick up a reduced price ticket from The Society of London Theatres' cut-price ticket booth, **tkts**, in the clocktower building on the south side of Leicester Square (open Mon–Sat 10–7, Sun noon–3:30). There is a service charge of a few pounds and tickets are for a performance on that day. For a popular show, this is often your only chance of getting a ticket: Be prepared to get there before noon to be as close to the front of the line as possible. There are other more expensive ticket booths in the square, so be careful to join the right line. Also, never

buy from scalpers who may approach you while standing in line. They are working illegally and the tickets could well be fakes.

Another option is the charity ticket hotline **West End Cares** (tel: 020 7833 3939). Tickets for popular West End shows, for example *Miss Saigon*, *Les Misérables*, *The Phantom of the Opera*, are available and the price includes a donation to AIDS charities.

Ticketmaster (tel: 0870 534 4444) can otherwise help you find seats. There is will be a service charge for credit card sales.

CLUBS

London is king of the hill as far as the music scene is concerned and in its clubs a wide spectrum of tastes are catered to, from mainstream rock acts, country and jazz, to techno, indie and hip hop sounds. The listings magazine *Time Out* (published every Tuesday) is the most authoritative and comprehen-

sive of all the London magazines. As music and themes vary from night to night, it is essential to check for up-to-date information. For example, **Heaven** (Under The Arches, Villiers Street, WC2, tel: 020 7930 2020. Tube: Charing Cross), a huge gay club with a laid back and friendly atmosphere, is also popular with straight men and women.

Other popular club venues worth checking out:

The Astoria (157 Charing Cross Road, WC2, tel: 020 7434 9592. Tube: Tottenham Court Road), a brilliant venue for up-to-the-minute sounds as well as rock and reggae.

Café de Paris (3 Coventry Street, W1, tel: 020 7734 7700. Tube: Piccadilly Circus), a glam dance hall, overlooked by a galleried restaurant.

The Rock Garden (6–7 The Piazza, Covent Garden, WC2, tel: 020 7240 3961. Tube: Covent Garden), a burger joint that is noted for showcasing new talent in a variety of musical areas.

Excursions

Kew

Kew is an excellent day out. Not only is it convenient – just a short boat or train ride from central London – but its highlight, the Royal Botanic Gardens, is the world's foremost botanical garden and one of the loveliest spots in the capital.

The Royal Botanic Gardens' 299 acres contain around 30,000 species of plants, including 13 species extinct in the wild. Keen botanists and gardeners will revel in the floral diversity, but non-experts can also easily savor the gardens' overall beauty. Visits outside the summer months can be especially rewarding – September through November produces wonderful fall colors, camellias bloom in January, and February through May sees the first blooms of spring. It would be easy to wander here for days, but to see the highlights visit the glasshouses in the order below. Their display boards, offer entertaining information about some of the plants.

The **Princess of Wales Conservatory** features ten computer-regulated climate zones. Stroll from orchids in the humid tropical zone to cacti in the dry tropical zone to appreciate the huge influence of climate on

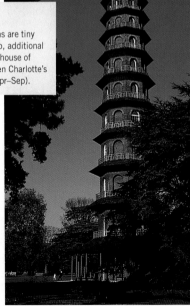

The ten-story Kew Pagoda. During World War II, the RAF drilled holes in its floors to test model bombs

Hidden Gems
• Tucked away within the gardens are tiny Kew Palace (open daily, Apr–Sep, additional small charge), once the summerhouse of George III, and the bucolic Queen Charlotte's Cottage (open Sat, Sun 10–4, Apr–Sep).

Previous page: The moat at Windsor Castle has been transformed into lovely gardens

Kew Gardens
☎ 020 8940 1171 (24-hour recorded information); www.kew.org ⏰ Daily 9:30–dusk (telephone for exact closing times). The glasshouses and galleries close earlier. Closed Jan 1, Dec 25 🍴 Several cafés and restaurants in the gardens and other options nearby 🚇 Kew Gardens 🚌 Kew Bridge 63, 391; also R68 (Sun only) For information on river trips to Kew from central London ➤ 102–103 💷 Moderate

floral types. The most bizarre plants are the lithops of
Namibia, also called "living stones," which are
indistinguishable from stones until they produce brilliantly
colored flowers.

The **Palm House** is a masterpiece of Victorian engineering,
constructed between 1844 and 1848 with some 16,000 sheets
of glass. Climb one of the wrought-iron spiral staircases to the
raised walkways to view its lush rainforest interior containing
tropical species such as coconut, banana and rubber from
across the globe, and don't miss the basement with its marine
plants and habitats, in particular the coral reef. Kew is one of
the few places in Britain with living coral, something that is
notoriously difficult to cultivate in captivity.

The **Temperate House** is the largest of the glasshouses
(590 feet by 138 feet). An elegant structure, it was begun in
1860, but work was stopped after the central block was fin-
ished and the building was not completed until almost
40 years later. Today its highlights are a Chilean wine palm,
planted in the mid-19th century and now one of the world's
largest indoor palms, and subtropical plants such as citrus
trees, tea trees and Himalayan rhododendrons.

Just behind the Temperate House is the **Evolution House**,
which traces the development of the most ancient plants. A
bubbling primordial sludge has been re-created, replicating –
it is thought – the earliest "soil." From here plant evolution is
traced from the first bacteria through algae, mosses and ferns
to conifers and flowering plants.

The ten-story **Pagoda** is perhaps the gardens' most
celebrated landmark. It was completed in 1762 for Princess
Augusta, the mother of George III, and at the time was the
most accurate reproduction of a Chinese building in Europe.

Top: The Palm
House at Kew
incorporates
16,000 panes
of glass and
took four years
to build

Above: Luxuriant
tropical plants
thrive in its
controlled
climate

Windsor

A visit to Windsor Castle is the obvious highlight of a trip to Windsor, but the town is attractive in its own right. There is also the chance to visit historic Eton College, traditionally a school for the sons of the rich and famous, and – a treat for the children – the modern theme park of Legoland.

Visitor Information Centre
✉ 24 High Street, Windsor
☎ 01753 743900
🕐 Daily including most public holidays; times vary throughout the year

Top tips
• The Changing of the Guard takes place at 11 am daily (except Sundays) from April through June and on alternate days for the rest of the year.

• Buy a guidebook on the way in, as very little is labeled.

Eton College
☎ 01753 671177
🕐 Daily 2:30–4:30 school term time, 10:30–4:30 school vacation time, Apr–Sep
💷 Inexpensive; tours moderate

Windsor Castle
☎ 01753 831118 (24 hour) or 01753 869898; www.royalresidences.com 🕐 Daily 9:45–5:15 (last admission 4), Mar–Oct; 9:45–4:15 (last admission 3) Nov–Feb. Closed Good Fri, Easter Sun morning, Dec 25–6, Service for the Order of the Garter in Jun. St. George's Chapel closed to visitors Sun. Subject to full or partial closure at other times 💷 Expensive (reduced price on days of partial closure)

Legoland Windsor
✉ Winkfield Road
☎ 08705 040404; www.legoland.com
🕐 10–6 (or dusk if earlier) mid-Mar–end Oct; (also daily 6–8 mid-Jul–early Sep)
💷 Expensive (2-day tickets available)

Windsor Castle

Windsor Castle looks the part of a castle to perfection, with towers, turrets, battlements and even uniformed soldiers on guard. It possesses a grandeur that far outshines that of Buckingham Palace (➤ 50–51). Britain's largest inhabited castle, Windsor was founded by William the Conqueror in about 1080, when it formed part of the defenses around London. In time it became a royal residence, partly because of the opportunities for hunting afforded by the surrounding countryside. Henry I had quarters in the castle in 1110, and almost 900 years later the sovereign is still resident. Queen Elizabeth II spends most weekends here, as well as much of April and June.

A fire on the night of November 20, 1992, probably started by the heat of a spotlight too close to a curtain, destroyed much of the castle's interior. Several State Rooms, including St. George's Hall, the Grand Reception Room, the State Dining Room and the Crimson Drawing Room were damaged. The fire burned for 15 hours and it took over 1.5 million gallons of water to extinguish it. Restoration took five years and cost $60 million, most of which was met by the Royal Family with money earned from the annual opening of Buckingham Palace and visitor admissions to the precincts of Windsor Castle.

Left: Windsor Castle is an imposing sight, especially from the Thames

Above: Henry VIII's gate

Areas of the castle open to the public include the State Rooms (all year), Semi-State Rooms (October through March only) and St. George's Chapel (daily, all year except Sundays). All are grand and all are worth seeing, their vast array of treasures embracing fabulous Gobelin tapestries, ornate antique furniture and paintings by artists such as Van Dyck, Rubens, Gainsborough, Dürer, Rembrandt, Reynolds and Canaletto.

The castle tour follows a set route, the key highlights of which are as follows:

Queen Mary's Dolls' House is an entire house built on a scale of 1:12. Look especially for the tiny leather-bound books in the library, and the vacuum cleaner, faucets, crockery, kitchen equipment, the miniature works of art on the walls, and a sewing machine that actually works.

The **Grand Staircase** and **Grand Vestibule** provide a magnificent introduction to the State Rooms. Both are lined with statues, firearms, armor and huge cases filled with miscellaneous treasures – among them, in the Grand Vestibule, the bullet that killed Admiral Lord Horatio Nelson at the Battle of Trafalgar in 1805 (currently on display at the National Maritime Museum in Greenwich ➤ 179).

The opulent **Grand Reception Room** was designed for King George IV, a monarch with a passion for ornate French design, which is why everything from walls and ceiling to furniture and chandeliers is intricately gilded and adorned.

St. George's Hall – superbly restored since the 1992 fire – is the grandest of the castle's rooms. At over 115 feet long, it is impressive for its size alone, but is also remarkable for its decoration – crests, busts and suits of armor – and the wonderful oak hammerbeam roof. Notice the King's Champion mounted on horseback on the balcony at the far end – as fine and dignified a display of armor as you'll see anywhere.

Ten monarchs are buried in **St. George's Chapel**, a beautifully decorated space distinguished, among other things, by its choir stalls, altar and gilded vaulting. It also contains Prince Albert's Memorial Chapel, built in memory of Victoria's beloved husband who died at Windsor in 1861. It's a startling piece of work, laden with statues, Venetian mosaics, inlaid marble panels: Albert himself is depicted in medieval armor, with his favorite dog, Eos, at his feet.

St. George's Chapel, the burial place of ten British monarchs, including the executed Charles I

Windsor

If you've more time to spend in the area, **Eton College** lies a 15-minute walk across the river from Windsor. One of Britain's oldest private schools, Eton was founded in 1440, and pupils still wear formal dress. Today it is highly prestigious; most pupils come from rich and influential families. More than 18 of Britain's prime ministers were educated here. The schoolyard, oldest classroom, museum and chapel are open to the public, and afternoon guided tours are available.

Legoland Windsor, a popular theme park just 2 miles from the town center, is ideally suited to those with younger children. It mixes rides and displays with constructions made from the popular Lego bricks – including models of famous buildings from around the world – together with live-action shows. A half-hourly shuttle bus operates to Legoland from stops close to Windsor and Eton Central and Riverside train stations (tickets including admission, shuttle bus and rail travel are available from most major train stations in Britain).

Getting There

Windsor is 21 miles west of London.

Train (☎ 0845 484950) Direct trains to Windsor and Eton Riverside from Waterloo Station, every 30 min. Journey time approximately 55 min. From Paddington Station to Windsor and Eton Central, changing trains at Slough, every 30 min. Journey time approximately 40 min.

Bus (☎ 0870 608 7261) From Victoria Coach Station, journey time 75–90 min. Telephone for times.